马鞍山文物聚珍

马鞍山文物聚珍

顾　　问：李修松　张敬国　贺云翱

主　　编：王俊

副 主 编：周雪梅　李敬华

撰　　稿：(以姓氏笔画为序)

　　　　　王　俊　吴志兴　李　军

　　　　　李敬华　陈　盈　周雪梅

　　　　　罗海明　郎　俊　费小路

　　　　　栗中斌　钱兵兵

绘　　图：徐红霞　王立新

拓　　片：费小路　王立新

英文翻译：江卫艺

临　　摹：张　捷　费小路

摄　　影：孙之常　赵　勇

文物修复：苗　杰　于　志

文　　印：王　菡　王　娟　江　晨

　　　　　闫辰浩

编目核对：李敬阳　陈晓艳　张厚金

马鞍山文物聚珍

TREASURE COLLECTION OF CULTURAL RELICS OF MA'ANSHAN

马鞍山市文物管理所·马鞍山市博物馆 编

王 俊 主编

文物出版社

序

　　提起马鞍山，人们以前首先想到的是：一座新兴的钢城。然而，在市委、市政府的高度重视和大力支持下，经过历史文化（文物）工作者的长期发掘、整理、保护和研究，如今展现在人们面前的是一个有着悠久历史和丰厚文化的地区。仅就文物来说，马鞍山已成为文物资源大市。

　　马鞍山的文物遗存分布相当密集，在全市1686平方公里的范围内已发现古墓葬、古建筑和其他名胜古迹140多处，其中国家、省、市、县级文物保护单位43处，将该市的历史上溯至5300年前的新石器时代。古遗址，已发现烟墩山、五担岗、邓家山、卞家山、荒庙墩、戴山、釜山、钓鱼台、船墩山等20多处新石器时代至商周时期的遗址；古城址，有古老的丹阳城遗址和始建于三国时期的姑熟城遗址以及始筑于东晋时期的牛渚城遗址；古建筑遗址，有昭明太子阁、凌云塔、彩虹桥、化城寺、谢公祠、虞公祠等多处；现保存较完整的古建筑，有名列沿江三楼一阁的太白楼建筑群，还有娥眉亭、济美坊、黄山塔、金柱塔、叶家桥、赤乌井、广济寺等多处。此外，还有古窑址以及众多的石刻、碑刻等。值得注意的是，马鞍山历史上因位于六朝古都南京的郊区，山水秀丽，环境幽雅，风水甚佳，所以这一带的六朝古墓相当多。其中重要的如东吴朱然家族墓（全国重点文物保护单位）、东吴宋山墓、东吴佳山墓、西晋霍里纪年墓、东晋谢沈墓、东晋孟府君墓、东晋林里纪年墓，以及其他一系列的古墓群、古墓葬等。更有唐代李白墓名闻遐迩，明代陶安墓、明代花云墓等也颇有价值。

　　上述墓葬中出土了大量的石器、陶器、瓷器、青铜器、漆木器、书画、玉器等，其中以青瓷和漆木器最为精美。青瓷大多出土于六朝墓葬，器形多样，工艺高超，具有重要的文物价值和历史文化价值。漆木器主要出土于朱然墓（该墓共出土80余件漆器），在全国产生很大影响，其中犀皮黄口羽觞、季札挂剑漆盘、宫闱宴乐图漆案等十分珍贵。这些文物反映的历史文化信息准确，极具研究价值。

　　从经济发展来看，马鞍山以钢铁生产为龙头的经济发展速度很快，目前已经成为安徽省的排头兵。然而，从文化资源的可持续发展来看，上述文物资源对马鞍山极为珍贵。第一，它以丰富的物质文化遗产的事实正在改变人们心目中对马鞍山钢城的单一形象，该市的文化品位正在得到质的提升。第二，可以结合对文物的利用，通过建设博物馆、文化馆、文化公园、文化广场等营造高雅的文化环境，从而优化城市发展环境，提高招商引资的吸引力，招来更多的投资者建设马鞍山。第三，可逐步将这些文物资源转化为旅游资源和文化产业资源，就是说可以利用文物结合当地山水风物发展旅游，通过一定的创意发展相关的文化产业，从而带动商业、房地产业、文化娱乐业、饮食服务业的发展，从而促使马鞍山的产业结构得到合理调整，确保经济社会全面、协调、可持续发展。

要实现上述目标，就必须要按照文物工作方针，对这些文物真正做到有效保护，合理利用。而做好文物资料的梳理、整合、出版、宣传工作，是一个十分重要的环节，也是实现上述目标必不可少的基础工作。

故此，马鞍山市博物馆的同仁们，顺应时势，扎实工作，在做好文物的鉴定、建帐、建档的基础上，予以认真梳理，整理了大量的资料。再通过分析研究，精挑细选，编辑成书，取名《马鞍山文物聚珍》。

本书共收录了150件文物精品，编者在编选时，力图做到种类丰富、主题突出。细细品味，不难发现，本书具有以下特点：

一是时代跨度较大。既有史前时期先民的文化遗存，如新石器时代的玉人、石钺等，也有商周时期直至明清时期的陶器、瓷器、青铜器、漆木器、玉器等文物精品，从一定程度上可以说是一部图像化了的马鞍山市文明发展史。

二是地域特色鲜明。所选文物中六朝文物占了70%左右，其中尤以六朝青瓷居多，与马鞍山的馆藏情况基本吻合，充分体现了马鞍山市博物馆立足六朝文物的办馆宗旨。

三是充分体现考古发掘成果。所选文物大部分是历年来考古发掘出土的，如漆木器多来自于被誉为八十年代十大考古发现之一的东吴大将军朱然墓，这些文物具有极高的历史、科学和艺术价值。

四是内容翔实，品位高雅。书中以高标准的精美图片配以翔实的文字说明，并以中英文对照的形式展现出来，具有较高的研究价值、收藏价值及艺术观赏价值。

感谢本书的策划者和编辑者奉献出这么好的精神食粮，同时也希望马鞍山的文博工作者在文物的保护和利用方面做出新的成绩，不断开创文物工作的新局面。

李修松
2006年4月24日

Preface

When Ma'anshan was mentioned in the past, what first came into people's mind was that it was an emerging city of steel, under the great importance attached and vigorous support given by the municipal committee of the Chinese Communist Party and the municipal government through the long-term excavation, arrangement, protection and research done by workers and history and culture(cultural relics), the city has turned into an area boasting a long history and profound culture. Only seen from the viewpoint of cultural relics, it can be named as a city with rich resource of cultural relics.

The immovable cultural relics of Ma'anshan are densely distributed. Within the 1,686 square kilometers area of the city, more than one hundred and forty ancient tombs, ancient architectural structures, and other scenic spots and historical sites have been discovered. Among these, forty-three are units of cultural relic preservation at state, province, city and country level, which trace the city's history back to the New Stone Age of 5,300 years ago. In terms of ancient sites, over twenty sites belonging to the New Stone Age and the Period of Shang and Zhou Dynasties have been discovered, including the Mount Yandun, the Hummock Wudan, the Mount Dengjia, the Mount Bianjia, the Mound Huangmiao, the Mount Dai, the Mount Fu, the DiaoYu Tai, the Mount Chuandun, etc. In terms of ancient city sites, there are the age-old site of Danyang City, the site of Gushu City which was first established in the period of Three Kingdoms, and the site of Niuzhu City which was first built in the period of Eastern Jin Dynasty. In terms of sites of ancient architectural structures, there are many ones including the Zhaoming Pavilion for Crown Prince, the Lingyun Tower, the Caihong Bridge, the Huacheng Temple, the Xiegong Ancestral Temple, the Yugong Ancestral Temple, etc. In terms of ancient architectural structures, there is the architectural complex of Tower of Li Bai which ranks first among the three towers and one pavilion along the Yangtze River, and there are also the Emei Pavilion, the Jimei Archway, the Huangshan Tower, the Jinzhu Tower, the Yejia Bridge, the Chiwu Well, the Guangji Temple and so on. Besides, there are ancient kiln sites which are of rich contents, and there are numerous stone inscriptions and inscribed stone tablets. It is a remarkable fact that for in the history Ma'anshan used to located in the suburb of Nanjing, the ancient capital of Six Dynasties, which is endowed with beautiful hills and waters, elegant and quiet environment, and a good geomantic omen, there are quite a few ancient tombs of Six Dynasties in this area. Among these tombs, Tombs of Zhu Ran Family (National key cultural relic preservation unit), the Songshan Tomb of Eatern Wu Dynasty, the Jiashan Tomb of Eatern Wu Dynasty, the Huoli Tomb with specific building year of Western Jin Dynasty, the Xieshen Tomb, the Mengfujun Tomb, the Linli Tomb with specific building year of Eestern Jin Dynasty and other series of ancient burial sites and ancient tombs. Furthermore, the Li Bai Tomb is renowned all over the world, and the Tao'an Tomb and the Huayun Tomb are also quite valuable.

What directly related to the above-mentioned ancient sites and burial sites are a great number of stone implements, potteries, bronzes, lacquer and wooden wares, paintings and calligraphies, jade wares and so on which have been unearthed therefrom. Among these, celadon and lacquer and wooden wares are most noticeable. Mostly unearthed in tombs of Six Dynasties, the celadon, which has various shapes and superb workmanship, has significant value of cultural relics and historical and cultural value. Lacquer wares are mainly unearthed from Zhu Ran Tomb (more than eighty lacquer wares have been excavated here), which deeply impress the whole country. Among these lacquer wares, the Eared Lacquer Cup with Rhinoceros Leather Body, the Lacquer Tray painted with Ji Zha Hanging Sword, and the Lacquer Table painted with a Banquet Screen are very precious. For these cultural relics are all unearthed in this city, the historical and cultural information that they reflect is accurateand has great research value.

With regard to economic development, the economy of Ma'anshan, led by steel production, has been experiencing rapid development, and has been among the tops in Anhui

Province. However, in the respect of sustainable development, the above-mentioned resource of Ma'anshan relics is extremely valuable to the city. Firstly, it is changing the single image of Ma'anshan as a steel city in people's eyes with the fact of abundant cultural heritages, and it is elevating the cultural taste of the city qualitatively. Secondly, combined with the utilization of cultural relics, it can create a elegant cultural environment by building museums, cultural centers, cultural parks, cultural plazas and so forth, optimize the city's development, increase its attraction for investments, and invite more investors to construct the city. Thirdly, the resource of cultural relics can be gradually transformed into tourism resource and cultural industry resource, i.e. it can combine cultural relics with local landscapes to develop tourism and develop relevant cultural industries with certain originality. Thereby the development of commerce, real estate industry, cultural and entertainment industry, food and beverage service industry can be promoted. The industrial structure of Ma'anshan can consequently be properly adjusted and it can make the full, harmonious and sustainable development of the city's economy and society be ensured.

In order to the above goal, the city must truly and effectively preserve and reasonably use these cultural relics in accordance to the work policies of cultural relics, good arrangement, integration, publication and propaganda of the documents of cultural relics are not only a significant link but also a fundamental work which is indispensable to achieve the above goal.

Therefore, staffs of museum in Ma'anshan work in a down-to earth way in tune with the times. On the basis of well identifying, setting up accounts and filling the cultural relics, they have carefully arranged them and sorted out a great deal of data. Then they carefully selected, edited and published a book named "Treasure Collection of Cultural Relics of Ma'anshan".

One hundred and fifty elaborate works of cultural relics are included in this book. The editors tried hard to achieve rich variety and prominent theme while selecting and editing. If we carefully taste it, we will easily find the following characteristics of the book:

First, it has a long span of time. It not only has treasures left over by ancient people of prehistoric times such as jade human figures and the stone battle-axes of the New Stone Age, but also has fine works of potteries, porcelains, bronze wares, lacquer wares and jade wares from Shang and Zhou period to Ming and Qing period. To some extent, the book can be considered as a picturized cultural development history of Ma'amshan City.

Second, it has distinctive regional feature. Seventy percent of the cultural relics selected belong to Six Dynasties and among these celadon of Six Dynasties is predominant particularly. It generally tallies with the situation of collection of Ma'anshan museum and fully represents the purpose for establishing the museum based upon cultural relics of Six Dynasties.

Third, it fully demonstrates the harvest of archaeological excavation. For example, most lacquer wares are from the tomb of Zhu Ran, a great general in Eastern Wu Dynasty, which is reputed as one of the ten great archaeological finds in the 1980s. These cultural relics are all of extremely high historical, scientific and artistic value.

Fourth, the book has full accurate contents, and has refined taste. In the book, high-standard exquisite pictures are combined with word explanation, represented both in Chinese and in English. It has relatively high value of research, collection and artistic appreciation.

We appreciate the designers and editors for offering us such excellent mental pabulum, and at the time we hope that workers of cultural relics and museum in Ma'anshan will make new achievements in protection and utilization of cultural relics and continuously open up new prospects in work concerning cultural relics.

Li Xiusong

April 24th, 2006

序

安徽省马鞍山市从1956年正式立市迄今正好50年，是中国最年轻的城市之一，但正如我国绝大多数城市一样，她同样有着历史悠久的区域开发史和文化积淀过程，而这一过程在传统文献中很难获得把握，现代考古学和文博工作恰恰填补了这个空白。打开马鞍山市考古文博工作者编写的这部文物图录，我们立即就会发现，具体而形象的实物资料证明，马鞍山市至少已经拥有5000年以上的历史，这块土地上的先民曾创造过骄人的区域文化，而且这种创造又通过当代博物馆的收藏、研究、展示和不同形式的信息传播，在现代城市文明的创新发展过程中继续发挥着不可替代的作用。

文物是人类文化的载体和见证，通过本书收录的资料，我们可以从一个侧面领略马鞍山古代文化的某些重要的特征。

一是具有较为鲜明的地域性。无论是新石器时代的玉器、商周时期的青铜器，还是三国两晋南北朝时期及此后的陶瓷器和铜器，我们都能发现诸多具有一定个性的器物造型，如烟墩山遗址出土的玉人、经济技术开发区出土的商代青铜铙、五担岗遗址出土的绳纹陶双系罐和陶瓿、新桥乡塔桥村出土的三足承盘铜香熏、电磁线厂出土的东吴"丙午"铭错金银铜带钩、寺门口东吴墓出土的陶厕圈和青瓷鸡首罐、太白乡出土的东吴青瓷镇墓兽、东吴朱然家族墓出土的兽首人身镇墓兽、二钢厂东晋墓出土的青瓷狮形插座（烛台）等。这些器物虽然未必皆是本地制作，但由本地人使用所表现出的文化选择仍然凸显出地域的文化构成和文化倾向，在一定程度上印证了马鞍山地区在古代不同时期人们的生产水平、社会面貌、生活结构和精神需求。

其次是反映了马鞍山古代文化的位置和体系。马鞍山市地处长江南岸，特定的地缘和交通线路决定了她的本土文化与长江流域特别是长江中下游文化有着天然的联系。烟墩山出土的半镯形和半璧形两类玉璜与太湖流域和宁镇地区的崧泽遗址（上海）、南河浜遗址（浙江嘉兴）、草鞋山遗址（苏州）、营盘山遗址（南京）等出土的崧泽文化时期的同类玉器较为接近；五担岗遗址及博望等地出土的印纹陶器同属于长江下游地区的"湖熟文化"系统；六朝时期的青瓷器大多数为典型的（浙江）越窑产品，有的具有（江西）丰城窑（如东苑小区晋墓出土青瓷点彩钵及博物馆在本地征集的南朝青瓷六系盘口壶等）或（浙江）婺窑（如八亩塘晋墓出土的青瓷束口罐等）的特点。还有的遗物造型如东吴朱然墓出土青瓷香熏、佳山乡东吴墓出土的青瓷镇墓兽等与湖北鄂州东吴墓出土的同类器相当接近，而类似于佳山乡印山村出土的青瓷"白毫相"俑在湖北武汉和湖南长沙吴、晋时期的墓葬中也有发现；东吴时期朱然墓出土的部分漆器甚至来自于长江上游的蜀地。即使是唐宋时代的器物，如书中收录的唐代长沙窑黄釉条褐彩双系罐、黄釉褐彩注子、查湾出土吉州窑瓷枕以及一批具有北宋繁昌窑特点的青白瓷器等，也无不是产自长江流域的著名窑口。

站在现代的视角上，我们可以说古代马鞍山地区的文化始终是一个开放的体系，同时又带有强烈的长江流域的文化特色和本地区文化创造的印记。

三是昭示了马鞍山文化传承发展的连续性以及它与周边城市的密切关系。

本书收录的材料从5000多年前新石器时代的玉石器一直到明清时期的青花和彩瓷器，年代跨度大，种类多，但由于这些文物绝大多数都是本地出土，因而从时间序列上反映了该地区文化面貌从简单到复杂的发展脉络和不同时期前后承转起落的关系。如果把马鞍山市出土文物所体现出的文化发展阶段及其面貌放到全国的大背景下观察，它大体上符合中国大多数地区物质文化演变的一般规律，但是由于马鞍山市又具有特殊的地理位置和资源优势，它在文化传承方面还表现出不平凡的一面，特别是它与附近的南京在历史上形成了一种非同一般的联动关系，这在三国两晋南北朝时期的文物上表现得尤为明显。文献资料证实，马鞍山市区最早兴起的城邑是位于今采石矶及翠螺山一带的"牛渚（屯）"，早在东汉末年，孙策就在这里击败扬州刺史刘繇的势力，从而由此打开了在江东地区的决胜局面，直到西晋灭吴战役中，东吴丞相张悌、丹阳太守沈莹等也是以此为抵抗晋军的关键城垒。实际上，历史上南京一旦作为都城，马鞍山的地位就会立即上升，东吴时期著名将领周瑜、陆逊，东晋镇西将军谢尚等均曾在此镇守，保卫都城；隋将韩擒虎由此过江进兵灭陈；北宋大将曹彬攻克采石后灭南唐；元末朱元璋攻打集庆（今南京）也是从这一带过江北上。正因为此，马鞍山市与历史上的南京的关系可谓唇齿相依，休戚与共。翻检此书收录的诸多三国两晋南北朝时期的文物，它们在器类、造型、纹饰等包括精美程度方面，与南京出土的同类文物几乎是不分彼此，这在南京附近其他城市是较难见到的现象。这种现象也可以从南朝诗人谢朓与唐代诗人李白在南京与马鞍山和当涂一带活动的过程及形成的文化传承关系，乃至对后来产生的一系列历史影响上看出这两座城市之间深远的文化联系。它充分说明，马鞍山市的发展与周边城市特别是与南京的互动具有战略性和持久性的文化意义。

本书收录的文物荟萃了马鞍山市出土历代文物的精华，其多方面的学术价值有待各方面的专家进行研究。主持这本书编写的马鞍山市博物馆馆长和马鞍山市文物管理所所长王俊同志是位富有学养的文物考古学者，多年来她一直工作在文博第一线，发表过多篇文物考古方面的文章，对马鞍山地区出土的古代墓葬、铜器、瓷器、墓志等做过系统的研究。十多年前，我在南京博物院考古部及《东南文化》编辑部时，她就是我们学术上的合作者。这本书虽然以图为主，但选择的文物、阐述的文字等综合反映了王俊同志和马鞍山市博物馆其他同志多年来田野工作的成果和研究水平，凝聚着许多人的汗水。同时，通过这本书也让我们感受到马鞍山市有关领导多年来对文博事业的重视和大力支持！

保护文物不仅是为了保存历史，更是为了传承文化，这本图录用数千年的遗存见证着马鞍山本地曾经有过的文化业绩和长江下游区域不同城市与地区间文化的持续和共生共荣的关系，愿我们从历史的启迪中分享智慧和创造，为着共同美好的未来做好我们当前的事业。

贺云翔

2006年4月20日

于南京大学文化与自然遗产研究所

Preface

Ma'anshan city of Anhui province has been for 50 years so far since it was officially founded in 1956, probably it is one of the youngest cities in China, but just as most of the cities in our country, she also bears the centuries-old region development history and the process of cultural accumulation and sedimentation that is rather difficult to grasp in traditional literature, while modern archaeology and cultural museum work just fill up the blank. Open up the catalogue of cultural relic complied by archaeological and cultural museum workers in Ma'anshan city, we immediately find that the concrete and vivid materials in kind prove Ma'anshan city at least has a history of more than 5,000 years. The ancestors on this land used to create proud region culture, and this creation continually plays an irreplaceable role in the creative development process of modern urban civilization through the collection, demonstration and information spread in indifferent ways by contemporary museums.

Culture is the only creation by human beings, and the cultural relic is the carrier and witness of human civilization. With the information collected and recorded in this book, we can get some idea of certain important characteristics of ancient culture of Ma'anshan from one side.

Firstly, it has comparatively distinct regionality. No matter the jade articles in the New Stone Age and bronze articles in the period of Shang and Zhou Dynasties, or chinaware and bronze wares in the period of Three Kingdoms, Western and Eastern Jin, and Southern and Northern Dynasties and succedent dynasties, we can all discover lots of article shapes with certain individuality, for instance, the jade figure unearthed in the site of the Mount Yangdun, the bronze cymbals in Shang Dynasty unearthed in economic and technological development zone of Ma'anshan, the pottery jar with cord markings decoration, double ties and the ceramic steamer unearthed in the site of the Hummock Wudan, the bronze incense burner with a tray and three legs unearthed in the Taqiao village of Xinqiao countryside, the bronze belt hook with gold-silver inlay and inscription "丙午" ("bing wu")of Eastern Wu Dynasty unearthed in the electromagnetic line factory, the pottery hog pen and the celadon chicken-head pot unearthed in the Simenkou tomb of Eastern Wu Dynasty, the celadon beast guarding for guarding tomb of Eastern Wu Dynasty unearthed in the Taibai countryside, the celadon beast for guarding tomb with beast head and human body unearthed in Zhu Ran family grave of Eastern Wu Dynasty and the celadon lion-shape jack (candleholder) unearthed in the tomb of Eastern Jin Dynasty in the second steel factory, etc. Although not all these utensils are made in the local places, the displayed culture choice by the using of local people still reflect the regional cultural structure and tendency, and to some extent reveal and prove the living level, the social appearance, the living structure and the spiritual demand of people in different ancient times of Ma'anshan area.

Secondly, it reflects the position and system of Ma'anshan ancient culture. Ma'anshan city is situated at the south bank by Yangtze River, and the special geographic and transport line determines the natural connection between her native culture and that of Yangtze River drainage area, especially the middle and lower reaches of Yangtze River. Unearthed semi-bracelet and semi-annular shaped jade pendants in the site of Mount Yangdun are close to the jade articles of the same category unearthed in the Songze site (Shanghai), the Nanhebin site (Jiaxing, Zhejiang province), the Caoxieshan site (Suzhou), the Yingpanshan site (Nanjing), etc. in Taihu Lake drainage area and Ningzhen area of Songze Culture period; the printed-line pottery unearthed in the site of the Hummock Wudan and Bowang, etc. belongs to the "Hushu Culture" system of lower reaches of Yangtze River; most of the celadon stoneware in six-dynasty period are typical (Zhejiang province) Yue kiln productions, some of which have the characteristics of (Jiangxi province) Fengcheng kiln (for example, point-colored celadon earthen bowl unearthed in a tomb of Jin Dynasty in Dongyuan residential area and the celadon pot with dish-shaped mouth and six loop handle rings of Southern Dynasty collected in local place by museum, etc.) or (Zhejiang province) Wu kiln(for instance, the celadon jar contracted mouth in the tomb of Jin Dynasty in Bamutang, etc.). Other relic shapes such as the celadon incense burner unearthed in Zhu Ran tomb of Eastern Wu Dynasty and the celadon beast for guarding tomb unearthed in the tomb of Eastern Wu Dynasty in the Jiashan countryside, etc. are rather similar to the articles of the same type unearthed in a tomb of Eastern Wu Dynasty in Ezhou, Hubei province, and there's also some discovery of the celadon "Baihaoxiang" figureine in the tomb of Wu and Jin periods in Wuhan, Hubei province and Changsha, Hunan province, which is similar to that unearthed in the Yinshan village, Jiashan countryside; parts of the lacquers unearthed in Zhu Ran tomb of Eastern Wu Dynasty are even from Shu place in the upper researches of Yangtze river. Even though the articles belong to Tang and Song Dynasties, none of them is not produced in famous kilns of the drainage area by Yangtze River, for example, the yellow-glazed jar with two loop handle rings and brown stripe design by Changsha kiln in Tang Dynasty and the yellow-glazed water dropper with decoration in brown, the porcelain pillow by Jizhou kiln unearthed in Zhawan and a batch of blue and white stoneware with characteristics of Fanchang kiln in Northern Song Dynasty, etc., all of which are collected in this book.

Standing on the modern angle of view, we can say that the culture of ancient Ma'anshan area is always an open system, and meanwhile brings along strong cultural features of the drainage area by Yangtze River and impression of the creation of local culture.

Thirdly, it makes clear to all that the transferring, inheriting and developing continuity of Ma'anshan culture and its close relationship with the surrounding cities. The materials collected and recorded in this book range from the jade and stone articles in the New Stone Age more than 5,000 years ago to the blue painting and colorful porcelains in Ming and Qing Dynasties, with a great span of years and various categories. But because most of these cultural relics are unearthed in local place, therefore, they reflect the local cultural appearance, the developing venation from simple to complicated and the relationship of ups and downs either forward or backward in different periods by time sequence. If the cultural developing period and its appearance revealed by the unearthed cultural relics of Ma'anshan city are put to observe under the big background of the entire country, it complies with the general evolutive rule of substantial culture in most of the Chinese area in principle; however, owning to the special geographic position and resource advantage of Ma'anshan city, it gives an outstanding performance in the aspect of transferring and inheriting culture, and especially it forms an unusual link with neighboring Nanjing in history, which is obviously displayed by the cultural relics in the period of Three Kingdoms, Eastern and Western Jin and Southern and Northern Dynasties. Literature materials prove that the earliest arisen city in Ma'anshan downtown area is located in the "Niuzhu(dun)" of Caishiji and Cuiluo mountain area. Early in the late years of Eastern Han Dynasty, Sun Ce triumphed over the force of Liu You here, feudal governor of Yangzhou, and from then on opened up the victory-deciding phase in East area of Yangtze River, until the battle that Western Jin annihilated Wu, the prime minister Zhang Ti and Danyang satrap Shen Ying of Eastern Wu Dynasty also took it as the crucial rampart to resist Jin army. In fact, once Nanjing is as the capital in history, the status of Ma'anshan would rise immediately. In the period of Eastern Wu Dynasty famous general Zhou Yu, Lu Xun, and west-town general Xie Shang of Eastern Jin Dynasty, all of whom used to guard here to protect the capital; Han Qinhu, general of Sui Dynasty, extinguished Chen by crossing the river from here; Cao Bin, general of Northern Song Dynasty, took up Caishi and then annihilated Southern Tang; at the end of Yuan Dynasty Zhu Yuanzhang attacked Jiqing (now Nanjing) also passed the river to the north from this area. Owing to that, the relationship between Ma'anshan city and Nanjing in history is well-nigh considered as close as lips and teeth and sharing weal and woe. Thumb through the culture relics in the period of Three Kingdoms, Eastern and Western Jin and Southern and Northern Dynasties collected and recorded in this book, they are almost as same as that unearthed in Nanjing in the aspects of article categories, shapes, line ornaments and the porcelain degree, which is a phenomenon that is seldom seen in the near and other cities. This kind of phenomenon can also be observed from the activity process and formed cultural transferring and inheriting relationship of the pots Xie Tiao of Southern Dynasty and Li Bai of Tang Dynasty in Nanjing, Ma'anshan and Dangtu area, and even realize the far-deep cultural connection between the two cities from the later a series of historical influences. It fully illuminates that development of Ma'anshan city and interaction with the neighboring cities especially Nanjing has strategic and constant cultural meaning.

The cultural relics collected and recorded in this book assemble the elite of the unearthed cultural relics for generations, and the multiphase academic value waits for the research by the expert of various aspects. Wang Jun comrade, the curator of Ma'anshan Museum and superintendent of Ma'anshan cultural relic management institute, who presides over the compilation of this book is a scholar of cultural relic archaeology with excellent academic culture. In many years she always works in the front of cultural museum, and has published many articles about archaeological cultural relic, as well as carries out systematic research of the unearthed ancient tomb funeral, bronze article, stoneware and tomb epitaph. More than ten years ago, when I worked in the archaeological department of Nanjing Museum and editing department of the magazine "the Southeast Culture". She was our academic partner. Although this book focusing on the picture, the selected cultural relic and interpretation character, etc. comprehensively reflect the result and research level of field working by Wang Jun comrade and other comrades of Ma'anshan Museum in so many years and embody the effort of many people. Meanwhile, through this book we can also feel the great support and recognition of the accomplishment of cultural museum by the concerned leaders of Ma'anshan city in these years.

Protecting cultural relics is not only for the preservation of history, but also to transfer and inherit culture. By the relics of thousand-year old, this catalog witnesses the past cultural achievement of the local place of Ma'anshan and culture persistence and relationship of mutual living and prosperity of different cities and regions in the lower reaches of Yangtze River. Wish we share the wisdom and creation from the enlightenment of history and do well of our current career for the mutual good future.

He Yun 'ao

April 20th, 2006

Research Institute of Cultural and Natural Heritage of Nanjing University

绪言

王 俊

马鞍山位于长江下游南岸，安徽省东部，与六朝古都南京为邻。在1600平方公里的土地上，分布着新石器中晚期至商周古文化遗址29处。全国、省、市、县重点文物保护单位43处。众多名胜古迹展示着城市悠久的历史和丰厚的文化底蕴。

烟墩山遗址的发掘表明，5300年前先民们就在此生息、繁衍、劳作，并创造了早期文明。在已发掘的950平方米的面积中，发现了一批新石器时代晚期至西周时期的重要文化遗址，出土有新石器时代的玉器、陶器、石器和西周时期的陶器、石器、青铜器、原始瓷器等各类文物近400件。除豆、簋、鬲等实用器外，有相当一部分为礼器，如石钺、玉璜等。其中一座新石器时代晚期的墓葬中出土玉人，立状侧面、戴冠、圆目、吻部突出、短颈、挺胸，背部有一方形缺口，玉人上下各对钻一小孔。整个玉人造型抽象与写实相结合。同时相伴出土的玉镯、玉项饰也十分精美，非一般人所使用。这批较高规格的新石器时代礼器的发现，进一步证明了马鞍山地区在当时便具有重要的宗教、政治地位。出土的生活用品在器形和纹饰上也反映出多种文化因素的影响，为我们探索马鞍山地区史前时期的文化交流传播提供了新的重要实物资料。

马鞍山作为六朝的京畿之地，濒临长江，地势险要，故有"六朝京畿天然屏障"之称。随着东吴政权的建立和此后东晋时期政治中心的南迁，北方士族大量南下，带来了先进的技术和充足的劳动力，马鞍山地区经济得到了进一步发展。据北宋《太平御览》卷一七〇，引《金陵记》记载："姑孰之南，淮曲之阳置南豫州，六代英雄选居于此，以斯为上地也"。这里也成为世家大族的魂栖之所。近二十年来马鞍山先后发掘六朝墓葬近百座，其中不乏高规格墓葬，如东吴朱然墓、宋山东吴墓等。

20世纪80年代初发掘的东吴大将朱然墓，是目前所知三国墓葬考古中唯一与《三国志·吴书》相印证的重要历史人物的墓葬遗存。朱然墓以其出土文物之珍贵，墓主身份之高，而成为80年代初中国十大考古收获之一。朱然墓穹窿顶的砌法已十分成熟，采用从四壁基墙的中部起，由两端向上斜砌，形成倒人字形壁面，至顶部合成方锥形。从力学角度观察，"四隅券进式"穹窿顶更为科学，它将墓顶上封土的重量均匀地传向四壁，有效提高了抗压能力。朱然墓成为长江下游吴墓中较早采用"四隅券进式"穹隆顶的实例。宋山东吴墓是目前长江下游已发掘的吴墓中规模最大的一座，长17.86米，结构复杂，由墓道、甬道、左右侧室、横前室、过道和单后室组成。营造相当讲究，前室与横室、横室与过道之间有四道石门，门把雕成辟邪式。它与朱然墓、朱然家族墓、东吴寺门口墓等构成了马鞍山东吴系列墓，为这一时间墓葬文化研究提供了重要资料。

马鞍山地区的文物具有鲜明的地域特点，六朝文物尤其是六朝青瓷占据了主流，也成为马鞍市博物馆的一大特色。这些文物多为墓葬中出土的随葬品，器形多样，工艺精湛，具有极高的历史、艺术价值。以青瓷器为例，几乎包括了这一历史时期常见的所有品种。如鸡首罐（壶）、盘口壶、唾壶、虎子、香熏、水盂、狮形烛台、盘、碗、钵、盏等日常生活用具，以及品种丰富的各类明器，如磨、灶、牛车、厕圈、禽舍、镇墓兽、青瓷堆塑罐等。其中不乏一些造型优美、纹饰精细、釉色匀润的器物。如朱然墓出土的青瓷卣形壶，朱然家族墓出土的青瓷羊，造型独特、典雅、纹饰精美。东苑小区东吴墓出土的虎子，构思巧妙，整体造型追求与虎形相似，犹如一只仰天咆哮的猛虎，写实生动，栩栩如生，凸显了东吴时期制瓷工艺的精湛。这一时期青瓷装饰风格的一个显著变化就是在器物上贴塑一些图案，其中以铺首最为常见。青瓷三足樽、青瓷奁均在肩部或腹部对称贴塑三个衔环铺首，青瓷卣形壶，肩部对称贴塑四个铺首，其中一对羊形铺首有两角，另一对铺首较小，紧贴在壶壁上，甚为独特。

从随葬的青瓷器所占比重变化中，我们可以看出，三国两晋时期，质朴、明洁的青瓷器逐步取代了汉代流行的漆木器、青铜器。但部分青瓷器在造型、纹饰上仍然承袭了汉代风格，如卣形壶、三足樽、青瓷奁，基本是汉代铜器的式样。制瓷工艺虽难以达到象铜器那样精密的雕刻效果，但上述几件青瓷器式样优美、装饰复杂、釉色莹润，胎釉结合致密，具有独特的美感，反映了越窑在三国两晋时期已具有相当高的烧成技术及制瓷工艺。

鸡首罐作为盛酒（水）器，是三国两晋时期瓷器的一种新产品。考古界此前一直认为吴、西晋的鸡首罐（壶），鸡首不能倾注，只是一种装饰。而宋山东吴墓出土的两件青瓷鸡首罐，鸡有雌雄之分，鸡首与腹相通，充当流的作用，应是实用器。西晋时有一种鸡首壶，鸡首仅仅作为装饰，似无实用价值，应视为明器。鸡首罐（壶）发展到东晋，已形成鸡首有颈，与鸡首相对称的鸡尾也发展成为与盘口交接，从造型上更趋于美观。马鞍山地区历年来出土了大量六朝时期的鸡首罐（壶），它们形制多样，构思巧妙，演绎出不同时期实物造型的发展序列。

虎子是六朝时期富于变化的主要器形之一。马鞍山三国两晋墓中，出土了一些形状不同的虎子。三国时的青瓷虎子多似蚕茧形，但个别东吴墓中也出土了一些呈圆球平底状虎子，口部只有装饰简单的耳、鼻。有关虎子的用

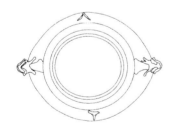

朱然墓出土的青瓷卣形壶

途应根据其形制、出土位置的不同来综合分析，其用途也应各异，不能简单地认为它只是溺器。

青瓷堆塑罐是三国两晋时期特有的一种产品。马鞍山出土的两件青瓷堆塑罐，腹部交错贴附麒麟、仙人骑马、羽人乘龙、佛像以及游鱼等水生动物。罐体上堆塑着复杂的楼宇、人物、动物形象。显示了烧造技术的成熟完善。同时也反映了汉末三国乃至西晋传入吴地的佛教，基本上依赖于中国传统文化的方术而生存，人们也将外来的佛视为神仙的方术之一种。从民俗的角度上看，人们认为"事死如事生"，将生前居住的庄园——堆塑在青瓷罐上，罐体贴塑的鱼、螃蟹、泥鳅等水生动物，更体现了江南水乡的特色，反映了这一时期贵族阶层的思想意识和他们的物质生活形态。

明器中用于辟邪的镇墓兽，在马鞍山六朝早期墓中也有发现。佳山东吴墓和朱然家族墓各出土一件。其中朱然家族墓出土的镇墓兽，兽面人身，两眼外凸，双耳居头顶，舌尖长至脚尖。据目前掌握的考古资料，长江中下游还未发现这一时期相同造型的器物，应是六朝早期难得的青瓷珍品。

漆木器是马鞍山市博物馆馆藏的一大亮点。东吴大将朱然墓出土的近80件漆器，品种繁多，包括案、凭几等家具，盒、壶等盛储器和碗、盘、耳杯等饮食器，以及妆奁器用、起居器用和文具。胎质有木胎、箧胎、皮胎，装饰工艺有描漆、戗金锥刻、雕刻镶嵌等。漆案上的绘画，内容丰富、题材广泛，对人物和动物的刻画，简率生动、布局饱满，如季札挂剑图漆盘，生动再现了《史记·吴太伯世家》所载的季札挂剑还愿、不失诚信的故事。宫闱宴乐图漆案，将帝王宴请诸侯王及其夫人观赏百戏的场面，形象地展示在案上，具有很强的艺术感染力。此外贵族生活图漆盘、童子对棍图漆盘、漆槅等均为三国漆器的经典之作。犀皮黄口羽觞，是饮酒用具，采用了由不同颜色的漆层构成天然流动图案的髹漆工艺。据文献记载，这种犀皮漆工艺可能发明于唐代，而朱然墓犀皮黄口羽觞的发现，将犀皮漆工艺的出现年代向前推进了近500年。这批漆器为研究魏晋时期美术史和漆工艺史提供了极其珍贵的实物资料。

青铜器数量不多，但馆藏的商周、汉晋等时代的青铜器质地优良，纹饰精美，具有浓郁的地域文化特色。马鞍山市经济开发区出土的一件商代青铜大铙，气势恢弘，纹饰精美，堪称镇馆之宝。铙的正鼓部饰勾连云纹和卷云纹组成的兽面纹等，与众不同的是，青铜铙除外壁布满纹饰外，在其腔内也同样铸有精美的勾连卷云纹饰。纹饰的主要作用是装饰，器内壁铸出如此精美的纹饰，显然具有一定的意义和作用。这件青铜铙是迄今为止我国所发现

朱然墓出土的瞿孝故事图漆盘

朱然墓出土的百里奚会故妻图漆盘

的唯一一件腔内有纹饰的青铜大铙，这为商周时期南方青铜铙的研究增添了新的内容，也为探讨我国南方早期青铜铙的年代、性质和功能增添了新的依据。

马鞍山馆藏的汉末至三国时期青铜器如三足承盘式香熏、错金银铜带钩、铜水注等制作精细，反映了当时的生活观念和艺术理念。

三足承盘式香熏，将神人、凤鸟和莲蕊装饰在一件器物上，有背光的造像，神人额中凸起的圈点，反映了东汉时期早期佛教对中国造像艺术所产生的影响。这两件香熏，造型优美、工艺精湛、使用方便，既是熏香除秽、净化空气的实用器，又是具有观赏价值的工艺品；错金银铜带钩，构思奇特巧妙，带钩俯视呈S形，一端似鹅头，弯曲作钩状，腹部雕刻成人抱鱼的形状，与"口含珠、手抱鱼、大吉"铭文相吻合。上述作品技法娴熟、雕刻精美，展示了三国时期青铜器的精湛工艺。

由于篇幅所限，马鞍山的文物不能一一介绍，我们希望通过这些有代表性的馆藏文物，让人们从中了解到马鞍山文物的地域特征，感受到马鞍山历史文化的魅力。

Preface

Wang Jun

Ma'anshan is located on the south band of the lower reaches of the Yangtze River, east of Anhui Province, bordering on Nanjing the capital of Six Dynasties. In its area of 1600 square kilometers, there are 29 ancient cultural sites from the middle and late period of the New Stone Age to Shang and Zhou Dynasty, and 43 key cultural relic protection units at state, province, city and county level. A great number of scenic spots and historical sites reveal a centuries-old history and rich cultural accumulations.

The site of Yandun Mountain shows about 5,300 years ago, our ancestors had lived, procreated and worked and created splendid cultures here. In an area of 950 square meters which has been excavated, a number of important cultural sites have been found, where many relics such as the jade articles, potteries and stone implements in the middle and late New Stone Age and the potteries, stoneware, bronzes, and primitive porcelains in Western Zhou Dynasty, etc. have been unearthed, altogether there are nearly 400 ones. In which, in addition to some practical wares, such as the dou (a vessel for severing food), gui (a utensil for severing food) and li (a kind of cooking utensil), there are also a good deal of ritual vessels, for example, the jade huang-pendants and stone battle-axes, and so forth. In a grave of the late period of the New Stone Age, a profile of a standing jade figure with a pointed mouth, short neck was excavated, which wears a hat, with its chest out and a square gap on the back, and a pair of small holes bored on the upper and lower part. It is a combination of abstractionism and realism. And the jade bracelets and jade necklaces unearthed at the same time are also very delicate and exquisite, which cannot be in possession of a common person. These ritual vessels further reveal the religious and political significance of Ma'anshan in the area at that time. And the shapes and patterns of the utensils also reflect that they had been influenced by many cultural factors and provide new and important tangible materials for the exploration of the culture exchange and communication in prehistoric period in Ma'anshan.

Ma'anshan, as an environ of the capital of Six Dynasties, lying in a strategic place bordering on the Yangtze River, has been regarded as "the natural protective screen of the capital of Six Dynasties" since times memorial. Along with the establishment of the regime of Eastern Wu and then the political center moving to the south in Eastern Jin Dynasty, a large number of the Shi Nationality people came to the south and brought advanced technology and sufficient labors, and the economy in this area developed further. "The Record of Jingling", the 170th chapter of "the Encyclopedia of Taiping "of Song Dynasty records:"In the south of the Gushu city and Huai river founded the southern part of Yuzhou. It is a superior place where heroes in Six Dynasties all chose to live here." It is also a place where eminent families and the nobility were buried. During the recent 20 years, hundreds of graves in Six Dynasties have been discovered successively, some of which are of high rank, such as the Zhu Ran's Tomb and the Songshan Tomb of Eastern Wu Dynasty, and so on.

The tomb of Zhu Ran, general in Eastern Wu Dynasty, is the only grave whose owner is an important historic figure in accordance with the one recorded in "The Romance of the Three Kingdoms·Annals of Wu" in all the graves of Three Kingdoms that have been discovered so far. Zhu Ran's Tomb becomes one of the ten great archaeological finds in the early 1980s in China for its precious relics and high social position of the burier. The technique of building on the dome has matured, adopting the way that from the middle of four foundation walls, which carries up slanting upwards, forming the walls surfaces of an upside character of "ren", and connects on the roof into a square tapered shape. Observing from the view of mechanics, the dome built in this way can uniformly distribute the weight of the mound heaped on the roof of the tomb and effectively improve the compression resistance. The Zhu Ran's Tomb is an earlier practice using "the way of carrying up from four sides" in graves of Eastern Wu in the lower reaches of the Yangtze River. The Songshan Tomb of Eastern Wu Dynasty, the largest one in the tombs of Eastern Wu Dynasty in the lower reaches of Yangtze River that have been dug up. It is 17.86 meters long and has a complicated and exquisite structure that is composed of tomb passage, paved path, right and left side rooms, horizontal and front rooms, passageway and single back room. There are four stone gates, the handles of which are caved into bixie (a fabulous beast that ward off evils). Together with the Tomb of Zhu

Ran's Family, Simenkou Tomb of Eastern Wu Dynasty, it constitutes a series of tombs of Eastern Wu Dynasty in Ma'anshan, and they provide significant materials for the research on the graves in this period.

The cultural relics in Ma'anshan have distinguished local features, a great many of which are of Six Dynasties, especially the celadon is the unique feature of Ma'anshan Museum. Most of the relics are funeral objects in various shapes and of refined and excellent techniques, and possess accurate cultural information and have great historical and artistic value. For instance, the celadon here contains almost all common kinds in this period, such as the cock-head jars (pots) , the tray-mouthed pots, huzi, the incense burners, the water droppers, the lion-shaped candleholders, plates, bowls, earthen bowls, cups, and other daily life utensils, as well as a various kinds of funerary wares, such as millstones, kitchen ranges, ox-carts, toilets, poultry houses, tomb guarding beasts, figured celadon jars, etc., some of which have exquisite patterns and bright and smooth colors. The celadon liquor pot in Zhu Ran Tomb and the celadon sheep in the Tomb of Zhu Ran's Family are all elegant and have unique shapes and delicate patterns. The huzi unearthed in the Eastern Wu Tomb in Dongyuan Residential Area is ingeniously structured, the overall shape of which looks like a roaring tiger, and clearly reveals the consummate crafts in Eastern Wu. That a remarkable change of the celadon decoration style in this period is that some patterns, especially the knocker-holder, is stuck and carved on the vessels. The celadon tripod cup, celadon mirror cases all have three symmetrical rings of knocker-holder on the shoulder and belly. The celadon liquor pot has four symmetrical knocker-holders on the shoulder, one pair of sheep-shaped knock-holders having two horns, the other pair which are comparatively smaller sticking closely to the wall of the kettle, which are extremely unique.

From the proportion variation of celadon buried along, we can see that during the period of Three Kingdoms and Two Jin Dynasties, celadon, with the advantage of simplicity, clearness and succinctness took the place of lacquers and bronze wares which were popular in Han Dynasty. However, some celadon wares still inherited the style of Han Dynasty in patterns and decorations. For example, liquor pots, tripod cups and mirror cases are basically in the style of bronze wares of Han Dynasty. Generally speaking, the carving workmanship of porcelain can hardly be as precise as bronze wares, but these pieces of celadon wares have beautiful styles, complex decorations, bright and smooth glaze colors, and tightly combined glazes, which represents that Yue Yao had already had fairish firing technique and workmanship of porcelain in the period of Three Kingdoms and Two Jin Dynasties.

The cock-head jar (pot), as a container for alcohol (water), was a new product developed during the period of Three Kingdoms and two Jin Dynasties. It was considered that the cock-head jar (pot) could not be used for pouring liquids but only for decoration. In the two cock-head jars (pots) unearthed from the Songshan Tomb of Easteyn Wu Dynasty, the chicken has sexual difference. The head and belly are open to each other for the function of stream. They should be applied. There was a kind of cock-head jar in Western Jin Dynasty. The cock head was just for decoration. It seemed that it was not applied. It should be regarded as articles to be for the dead. As the cock-head jar (pot) developed into Eastern Jin Dynasty. The cock head had a neck and the cock tail which was symmetrical with the head also developed into handle and connected with the mouth. In terms of patterns, it became more beautiful and practical. Over years, a great number of cock-head jars (pots) belonging to Six Dynasties have been unearthed in Ma'anshan area. They have various shapes and structures and ingenious designs, displaying the development sequence of patterns in different times.

Huzi (a kind of articles buried together with the dead) is among the major wares of the Six Dynasties with rich varieties. Some huzi with different shapes were unearthed from tombs of the Three Kingdoms and Two Jin Dynasties in Ma'anshan. Celadon huzi of Three Kingdoms are most in the shape of pod. However, in very few tombs of Eastern Wu Dynasty, some huzi unearthed have the shape of round ball and flat bottom and there are only simply decorated ears and noses at the mouth. The use of huzi which should be comprehensively analyzed according to the shape and the structure and the location of excavation and it cannot be simply regarded as chamber pot.

The figured celadon jar is a product peculiar to the Three Kingdoms and Two Jin Dynasties. On the two figured celadon jars unearthed in Ma'anshan, figures of unicorn, celestial being riding horses, man with feather riding dragon, figure of Buddha, swimming fish and other aquatic animals interweaving on the belly. The body is sculptured with complex figure of buildings, characters and animals. It shows the maturity and perfectness of firing technique. Meanwhile, it represents that the Buddhism, which was introduced into Wu area of Three Kingdoms at the end of Han Dynasty and even Western Jin Dynasty, developed relying on the arts of necromancy of Chinese traditional culture. People regarded the exotic Buddhism as one kind of supernatural beings' arts of necromancy. From the viewpoint of the folk custom, people thought "to die is to live" and sculptured the mansion where they livedssssswhen they were alive on the celadon jars. Fish, crabs, loaches, and other aquatic animals sculptured on the jar body further represents the characteristic of the south of the lower reaches of the Yangtze River, a region of rivers and lakes. They reflect the ideology and the form of material life of aristocratic stratum in that period.

Tomb guarding beasts of articles to be for the dead used for warding off the evil were also discovered in the tomb of early Six Dynasties in Ma'anshan. Two pieces were unearthed from Jiashan Tomb of Eastern Wu Dynasty and Zhu Ran's Family Tomb each. Among these, the tomb guarding beast unearthed from Zhu Ran's Family Tomb has beast's face and man's body, two outward bulging eyes, two ears on the top of head, and a long tongue reaching the tiptoe. According to present archaeological material that have been obtained, no ware with the same pattern has been found in the middle and lower reaches of Yangtze River. It should be a rare celadon treasure of early Six Dynasties.

Lacquer and wooden ware is a spotlight of the collection of Ma'anshan museum. In particular, near eighty lacquer wares unearthed from Zhu Ran's Tomb have wide variety, including furniture such as lacquer table and pingji (a kind of small-sized furniture that people lean against when sitting on the ground in ancient China), containers such as ge (a utensil for holding food in ancient China), boxes, kettles, wares for eating and drinking such as bowls, plates, eared cup, utensils for dressing and making-up, utensils for daily life and writing materials. The roughcast has wooden, thin bamboo strip and hide. In terms of decoration techniques, lacquer paintings, inlaying with gold and carving with awl, etc. The pictures on the lacquer table have rich contents, wide subject matters, and harmonious proportion of head, limbs and body with regard to carving and painting of figures. The figures have various gestures. For example, the Lacquer Tray Painted with Ji Zha Hanging sword combines expression with reality and vividly represents the story that Ji Zha hung a sword to fulfill his promise and maintained his creditability. The Lacquer Table Painted with a Banquet Scene shows the scene that the emperor feasted dukes, and princes and their wives watched acrobatics, which has very strong artistic appeal. In addition, Lacquer Tray Painted with Aristocrats' Life, Lacquer Tray Painted with Two Boys Wielding Sticks with Each Other and lacquer ge are all classics of the period of Three Kingdom. Eared Lacquer Cup with a Rhinoceros Leather Body adopts the technique of coating with lacquer which perhaps invented in Tang Dynasty, and it traces the history of this technique ahead of five hundred years. This batch of lacquer wares provides extremely valuable object materials for researching the history of art and lacquer techniques of Wei and Jin period.

Though in small quantity, the collection of bronze wares of Shang and Zhou, Han and Jin period are of high quality and have exquisite decoration and strong local cultural features. The big bronze cymbal of Shang Dynasty unearthed in the economic development zone of Ma'anshan has grand majesty and elaborate decorations, which can be called the treasure that guards the museum. The front body of the bell-shaped gong is decorated with lines of beast face composed of lines moiré cloud and cirrus. What makes the bronze cymbal different from others is its cavity which is also drawn with exquisite lines of moiré cloud and cirrus besides the lines sprinkling on the outer wall. The major function of lines is for decoration. As to such fine lines decorated on the inner wall, it must have certain meaning and function obviously.

This bronze cymbal is the only one with lines of clouds decorated on the inner wall that been discovered in China up till now. It adds new content to the research of bronze cymbals of the south in the period of Shang and Zhou, and also provides new basis for the discussion of year, quality and function of bronze cymbals of the south in the early stage.

Bronze wares from the end of Han Dynasty to the period of Three Kingdoms collected in the museum of Ma'anshan such as tripod incense burners, bronze daigou (a kind of clasp on the waistband) inlaid with gold and silver and bronze shuizhu (a little water pot for adding water while Chinese ink is grinded) are made delicately, reflecting the idea of life and perception of art of that time.

The tripod incense burners, combining the decoration of the immortal, phoenix and lotus on one ware, the statue with back to the light and the protuberant dot in the middle of forehead reflect in the Eastern Han Dynasty the influence of Buddhism on the arts of statue of China in the early stage. These two pieces of incense burners have beautiful shape, masterly workmanship and are convenient to use. They are not only applicable wares for removing foul air with incense and purifying air, but also handcraft articles with high value of appreciation. The bronze daigou (a kind of clasp on the waistband) inlaid with gold and silver is ingeniously designed. It has the shape of "S" when looked down on. One end looks like goose head and bends with the shape of a hook and the belly is carved into the shape of man holding a fish, which tallies with the inscription of " bead keeping in mouth and fish holding in hand, it is very propitious". The whole piece has skilled technique and refined carving, representing the excellent technique of bronze wares of Three Kingdoms period.

Due to limitations on space, the cultural relics of Ma'anshan City cannot be introduced one by one. We hope that through these representative collected cultural relics, people can get a glimpse of the cultural relics' local features of Ma'anshan City and have a taste of the charm of historical culture of Ma' anshan City.

图版目录
CONTENTS

马鞍山文物聚珍

玉石器

JADE AND
STONE WARES

TREASURE COLLECTION OF CULTURAL
RELICS OF MA' ANSHAN

◎
第一部分

石 斧　新石器时代　高12.3厘米　刃宽7.3厘米
2003年马鞍山佳山乡烟墩山遗址出土
Stone axe　Neolithic period　Height12.3cm　Blade breadth7.3cm
Unearthed in 2003 from Yandunshan site at Jiashan countryside, Ma'anshan
石质坚硬，呈青灰色。通体磨光，器体呈梯形，双面弧刃。

石 铲 新石器时代　长12.9厘米　宽12.3厘米　孔径5.5厘米
马鞍山当涂县青山乡征集
Stone shovel　Neolithic period
Length12.9cm　Breadth12.3cm　Hole diameter5.5cm
Collected from Qingshan countryside of Dangtu county, Ma'anshan
石质坚硬，青灰色。通体磨光，呈舌形，弧刃，器身扁平，两
面对钻单孔，孔径较大，孔壁光滑。

石 钺　新石器时代　高14.0厘米　刃宽9.2厘米
2003年马鞍山佳山乡烟墩山遗址出土
Stone Yue-axe　Neolithic period
Height14.0cm　Blade breadth9.2cm
Unearthed in 2003 from Yandunshan site at Jiashan countryside, Ma'anshan
石质坚硬，麻灰色。通体磨光，弧刃，上部对钻圆孔。

石钺 新石器时代 高13.2~13.0厘米 刃宽9.2~8.6厘米
2003年马鞍山佳山乡烟墩山遗址出土
Stone Yue-axe Neolithic period
Height13.2~13.0cm Blade breadth9.2~8.6cm
Unearthed in 2003 from Yandunshan site at Jiashan countryside, Ma'anshan
两件。石质坚硬，呈黑色。通体磨光，弧刃，上部有对钻圆孔。

石锛 新石器时代 长9.8~6.5厘米 刃宽4.2~3.6厘米
2003年马鞍山佳山乡烟墩山遗址出土
Stone adz Neolithic period
Length9.8~6.5cm Blade breadth4.2~3.6cm
Unearthed in 2003 from Yandunshan site at Jiashan countryside, Ma'anshan
两件。石质坚硬，呈灰色。通体磨光，器体呈长方形，弧背出段，单
面刃。

玉 人　新石器时代　高3.6厘米　宽1.5厘米
　2003年马鞍山佳山乡烟墩山遗址出土
Jade human figure　Neolithic period
Height 3.6cm　Breadth 1.5cm
Unearthed in 2003 from Yandunshan site at Jiashan countryside，Ma'anshan
玉质，灰白色，受沁。雕刻人形，立状侧面，戴冠，圆目，吻部突出，
短颈，挺胸，背部有一方形缺口。上下各对钻一孔。

玉 璜　新石器时代　长6.8厘米　宽2.8厘米　厚0.3厘米
　2003年马鞍山佳山乡烟墩山遗址出土
Jade huang-pendant　Neolithic period
Length6.8cm　Breadth 2.8cm　Height 0.3cm
Unearthed in 2003 from Yandunshan site at Jiashan countryside，
　Ma'anshan
玉质，灰白色。半环形，器表光素无纹，两端各有一穿孔。

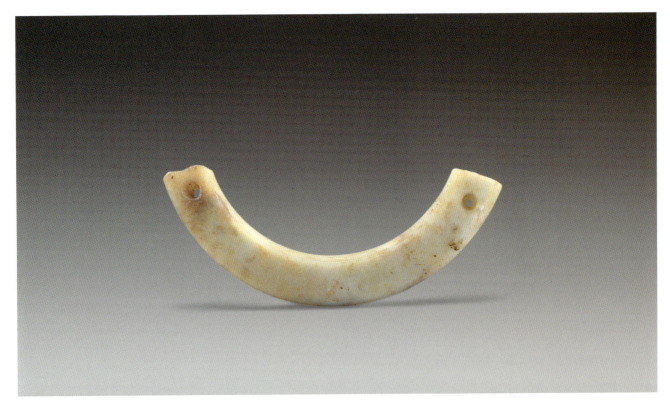

玉 璜　新石器时代　长5.6厘米　宽0.8厘米　厚0.3厘米
2003年马鞍山佳山乡烟墩山遗址出土
Jade huang-pendant　Neolithic period
Length5.6cm　Breadth 0.8cm　Height 0.3cm
Unearthed in 2003 from Yandunshan site at Jiashan countryside,
Ma'anshan
玉质，白中泛青，受沁。半环形，器表光素无纹，两端各有
一穿孔。截面不甚规整。

玉 璜　新石器时代　长6.0厘米　宽0.8厘米　厚0.3厘米
2003年马鞍山佳山乡烟墩山遗址出土
Jade huang-pendant　Neolithic period
Length6.0cm　Breadth 0.8cm　Height 0.3cm
Unearthed in 2003 from Yandunshan site at Jiashan countryside,
Ma'anshan
玉质，白中泛青，受沁。半环形，器表光素无纹，两端各有
一穿孔。截面不甚规整。

玉 镯　新石器时代　宽1.8厘米　内径4.2厘米　外径4.7厘米
2003年马鞍山佳山乡烟墩山遗址出土
Jade bracelet　Neolithic period
Breadth1.8cm　Inner diameter4.2cm　Outer diamter4.7cm
Unearthed in 2003 from Yandunshan site at Jiashan countryside,
Ma'anshan
玉质，白中泛青，受沁。环形，器表光素无纹。

玉 蝉　西汉　长5.2厘米　宽2.8厘米　厚1.2厘米
1996年5月马鞍山金家庄区寺门口汉墓出土
Jade cicada-shaped ornament　Western Han Dynasty
Length5.2cm　Breadth 2.8cm　Height 1.2cm
Unearthed in May, 1996 from Simenkou Tomb of Han Dynasty at Jinjiazhuang
district, Ma'anshan
羊脂玉。蝉形，纹饰刻画简洁。仅以几条阴线刻划，将蝉头、眼、身形表
现得完美逼真。

玉璏 西汉　长10.7厘米　宽2.5厘米　厚1.7厘米
1996年5月马鞍山金家庄区寺门口汉墓出土
Jade scabbard-buckle　Western Han Dynasty
Length10.7cm　Breadth 2.5cm　Height 1.7cm
Unearthed in May, 1996 from Simenkou Tomb of Han Dynasty at
Jinjiazhuang district，Ma'anshan
青白玉。正面剔地浅雕，一端刻有饕餮纹，背上纹饰以中轴线
分隔，左右对称，饰勾连云纹，线条精细流畅。

玉璏 西汉　长7.3厘米　宽2.0厘米　厚1.4厘米
1996年5月马鞍山金家庄区寺门口汉墓出土
Jade scabbard-buckle　Western Han Dynasty
Length7.3cm　Breadth 2.0cm　Height 1.4cm
Unearthed in May ,1996 from Simenkou Tomb of Han Dynasty
at Jinjiazhuang district，Ma'anshan
青玉，玉面泛浆有沁色。背面有浮雕蟠龙一只，龙身周围
衬托有数条阴刻纹饰。

玉 璏 西汉 长7.2厘米 宽1.9厘米 厚1.4厘米
1996年5月马鞍山金家庄区寺门口汉墓出土
Jade scabbard-buckle　Western Han Dynasty
Length7.2cm　Breadth 1.9cm　Height 1.4cm
Unearthed in 1996 from Simenkou Tomb of Han Dynasty at
Jinjiazhuang district, Ma'anshan
玉质，青色，长方形，受沁。长檐下垂内卷，短檐长伸斜前
下垂，器面刻浮雕神兽纹，浅刻浮雕下垂，辅以阴刻勾连纹。

滑石猪 西晋 高1.0厘米 长8.5厘米 宽1.9厘米
1988年马鞍山霍里镇晋墓出土
Steatite hog　Western Jin Dynasty
Height1.0cm　Length8.5cm　Breadth1.9cm
Unearthed in 1988 from a Western Jin Dynasty tomb at
Huoli town, Ma'anshan
一对。石质，灰色，猪身扁平较长，五官刻画简洁。

滑石墓志　东晋　长10.2厘米　宽7.7厘米　厚1.5厘米
1985年5月马鞍山雨山区出土
Steatite epitaph　Eastern Jin Dynasty
Length10.2cm　Breadth7.7cm　Height1.5cm
Unearthed in May,1985 from an Eastern Jin Dynasty tomb at Yushan district,
Ma'anshan
石质，长方形。正反两面阴刻文字，正面两行十字："弘农杨邵妻 济阳虞
道育"，反面三行十五字："太元廿一年丙申岁六月廿二日甲午"。

滑石猪 东晋 高3.3厘米 长10.3厘米 宽2.4厘米
1992年5月马鞍山慈湖乡东晋墓出土
Steatite hog Eastern Jin Dynasty
Height3.3cm Length10.3cm Breadth2.4cm
Unearthed in May,1992 from an Eastern Jin Dynasty tomb at Cihu
countryside, Ma'anshan
一对。石质，灰白色。器身圆浑较长，耳、鼻、嘴部刻划清晰，
嘴部圆形上翘，尾巴刻成"6"字形。

滑石猪 六朝 高2.9厘米 长9.5厘米 宽2.4厘米
马鞍山佳山乡六朝墓出土
Steatite hog Six Dynasties
Height2.9cm Length9.5cm Breadth2.4cm
Unearthed from a Six Dynasties tomb at Jiashan countryside, Ma'anshan
一对。石质，灰中泛红色。器身圆浑较长，用简洁细条刻划出五官、
四肢蜷曲作卧伏状。

抄手砚 北宋　长11.0厘米　宽2.5厘米　长沿宽7.0厘米　短沿宽6.4厘米
1987年马鞍山当涂县新市乡征集
Stone inkstone　Northern Song Dynasty
Length11.0cm　Breadth2.5cm
Collected in 1987 from Xinshi countryside of Dangtu county, Ma'anshan
石质，砚面呈梯形，面成弧形伸向短沿成砚池。砚底挖空呈箕形，底
面自右至左直书三行："福建武阳光泽郡邑、陈留和叔仪叔，政和伍
年三月三日交讫"。砚石质细腻致密，光滑柔润，造型既轻且稳，实
用雅观。

马鞍山文物聚珍

青铜器

BRONZE
WARES

TREASURE COLLECTION OF CULTURAL
RELICS OF MA'ANSHAN

◎

第二部分

青铜铙　商　高52.5厘米 长41.0厘米
宽26.6厘米 重54.0千克
2002年马鞍山经济技术开发区出土
Bronze Nao-instrument Shang Dynasty
Height52.5cm　Length41.0cm　Breadth26.6cm
Weight54.0kg
Unearthed in 2002 from a zone for economic and
technological development , Ma'anshan

钲部为合瓦形，上宽下窄，甬素面中空，与
腔体相通。钲的正鼓部饰由勾连云纹和卷云
纹组成兽面纹，左右侧鼓部饰对称的勾连云
纹。钲的中部以卷云纹分为左右两部分，四
周以联珠纹为界，内为阳线菱形雷纹，雷纹
内填阳线卷云纹，在云雷纹的中央有突起的
卷云纹，并围绕涡纹一起构成夔纹，两夔又
构成兽面的两目。钲的下部为卷云纹。铙侧
为卷云纹。腔内壁分为左右两部分，以直线
分为四组，内为勾连卷云纹。舞的内壁阴刻
勾连卷云纹。

青铜甬钟 西周 高35.0厘米
1977年6月马鞍山当涂县新市乡征集
Bronze YongZhong- instrument Western Zhou Dynasty Height35.0cm
Collected in June,1977 from Xinshi countryside of Dangtu county, Ma'anshan
甬作上小下大圆柱状，有旋，旋上附干，平舞。枚占全长的三分之一，
分三行六组，每组三枚。铣尖，长腔，于弧。舞、钲、篆、鼓饰窃曲纹。

青铜剑 春秋 长34.4厘米 宽3.6厘米
2002年马鞍山霍里镇五担岗遗址出土
Bronze sword　Spring and Autumn period
Length34.4cm　Breadth3.6cm
Unearthed in 2002 from Wudangang site at Huoli town,
Ma'anshan
斜宽从，前锷收狭，甚锋利。圆茎上有两道凸箍，
厚格，剑身有脊。

青铜鼎 西周~春秋 高15.0厘米 口径25.0厘米
马鞍山当涂丹阳镇征集
Bronze Ding-tripod　Western Zhou Dynasty — Spring and Autumn period
Height15.0cm　Mouth diameter25.0cm
Collected from Danyang town of Dangtu county, Ma'anshan
侈口，扁鼓圆腹，口沿下附一单耳，单耳与一腿对应，足呈蹄形，上
粗下细。肩饰回纹，腹部饰弦纹和勾连纹。

青铜提梁壶　东汉　高29.2厘米　口径8.0厘米
1996年8月马鞍山钢铁公司东汉墓出土
Bronze loop-handled pot　Eastern Han Dynasty
Height29.2cm　Mouth diameter8.0cm
Unearthed in August,1996 from an Eastern Han Dynasty tomb at Ma'anshan
Iron and Steel Corporation
壶有盖，扁腹，长条形足，肩腹之间对称置两凤形耳，两耳之间有链
状龙形提梁。

青铜弩机 东汉 郭长13.5厘米 望山长7.0厘米 悬刀长7.5厘米
1977年马鞍山当涂县新桥乡东汉墓出土
Bronze crossbow Eastern Han Dynasty
Length of guo (housing)13.5cm
Length of wangshan (a device similar to front sight of a gun)7.0cm
Length of xuandao (trigger,lit.,hanging knife)7.5cm
Unearthed in 1977 from an Eastern Han Dynasty tomb at Xinqiao
countryside of Dangtu county, Ma'anshan
弩机由郭牙、望山、悬刀组成，郭上有箭槽，机身刻有铭文：
"延喜四年十一月戊戌五年九月九日诏书选大后機（机）工柴初"。

三足承盘青铜香熏 东汉

高16.5厘米 熏径10.5厘米 盘径16.3厘米

1977年马鞍山当涂县新桥乡东汉墓出土

Bronze incense burner with a tray and three legs

Eastern Han Dynasty

Height16.5cm　Burner mouth diameter10.5cm

Tray diameter16.3cm

Unearthed in 1977 from an Eastern Han Dynasty tomb at Xingqiao countryside of Dangtu country, Ma'anshan

上、右两图的这件香熏，球面镂空，盖顶有立凤，展翅挺立。一神人双手向上，以仙药饲凤。神人背后有一仙鸟，鸟为卧状，凤的左右后各有一神人，跪姿、无头光，双手合揖。置龙首长柄，龙口张开，额顶前有两只卷曲角，曲颈，有鳞纹，下置三熊形蹄足。球体四周饰有莲蕊纹带。

三足承盘铜香薰 东汉

高15.0厘米 熏径12.0厘米 盘径15.2厘米

1977年马鞍山当涂县新桥乡东汉墓出土

Bronze incense burner with a tray and three legs

Eastern Han Dynasty

Height15.0cm　Burner mouth diameter12.0cm

Tray diameter15.2cm

Unearthed in 1977 from an Eastern Han Dynasty tomb at Xingqiao countryside of Dangtu country, Ma'anshan

左图的这件香薰，球面镂空，盖体分为三瓣，可开合。三兽形足，承盘有三乳突。盖顶中央一凤，凤足周围有莲蕊纹，凤侧有一神人手捧仙药。盖顶周围有花朵、仙鸟及四位神人。神人作跪姿，其中一人残缺，余三人额正中凸起，似为"白毫相"。其中二人双手拱在胸腹前，另一人左手平放胸前，右手上举至耳。

正方体，上刻"别部司马"四字。

青铜印　汉　长2.4厘米 宽2.4厘米
1998年征集
Bronze seal　Han Dynasty
Length2.4cm　Breadth2.4cm
Collected in 1998
正方体，上刻"别部司马"四字。

环绕式神兽青铜镜　三国·吴　直径12.4厘米　缘厚0.4厘米
纽径3.4厘米
1984年马鞍山雨山区朱然墓出土
Bronze mirror with gods and animals　Wu,Three Kingdoms Period
Diameter12.4cm　Height0.4cm　Knob diameter 3.4cm
Unearthed in 1984 from Zhu Ran Tomb at Yushan　district, Ma'anshan
青色，圆形。扁圆纽，圆纽座，主体纹饰为六神三兽一龙，可分四
组，两两对应。其中两组由两神像组成，另两组为一神一兽一龙，
神像居中，龙作遨游回顾状。主纹外有方枚和半圆枚各八个，相间环
绕，方枚上无铭文，半圆枚上有圆圈纹，向外有一周栉齿纹，近缘处
是一圈铭文带，三十四字，反书，字体难辨。

柿蒂八凤青铜镜　三国·吴　直径14.9厘米　纽径3.8厘米
1984年马鞍山雨山区朱然墓出土
Bronze mirror with eight phoenixes design Wu,Three Kingdoms Period
Diameter14.9cm　Knob diameter3.8cm
Unearthed in 1984 from Zhu Ran Tomb at Yushan district, Ma'anshan
青色，圆形。扁平圆纽，圆纽座。主体纹饰有四柿蒂形叶伸向镜缘，
叶间有八只凤鸟，两两相对。振翅翘尾。凤鸟体下间饰一圆点纹。
四叶内各有一形态各异的龙，或遨游或回顾。近缘处是内向十六连弧
纹圈带，内有虎、龙、鸟、兔等神禽异兽，还有一"出"字图案，素缘。

夔凤青铜镜　三国·吴　直径15.1厘米 纽径2.9厘米
1998年马鞍山金家庄区寺门口东吴墓出土
Bronze mirror with Kui- phoenix design　Wu,Three Kingdoms Period
Diameter15.1cm　Knob diameter2.9cm Height0.3cm
Unearthed in 1998 from Simenkou Tomb of Eastern Wu Dynasty at Jinjiazhuang district, Ma'anshan
圆形，圆纽，镜面微鼓，内区饰夔纹、凤纹，宽素带。

环状乳神兽青铜镜 三国·吴 直径14.2厘米 纽径2.2厘米
缘厚0.4厘米
1998年马鞍山金家庄区寺门口东吴墓出土
Bronze eight-nippled mirror with gods and animals design
Wu,Three Kingdoms Period
Diameter14.2cm Knob diameter2.2cm Height0.4cm
Unearthed in 1998 from Simenkou Tomb of Eastern Wu Dynasty at
Jinjiazhuang district, Ma'anshan

圆形，圆纽。镜面微鼓，纽外一圈连珠纹，内区饰东王公、西王母、伯牙奏琴、兽首等。四神和四兽相间环绕，其间有八枚环状乳。外有一周半圆方枚带，每一方枚中有四字："吾作明镜，幽谏三商，宜周册昌，□□□□，日月举宫，众申具周，有青西具，直角灰目，富贵安吉，具示巨车，车吴里豆，其巿吉羊。"镜缘纹饰为神人捧日，六龙驾车的日神出游图，云纹缘。

"五凤二年"环绕式神兽青铜镜　三国·吴　　直径12.4厘米　缘厚0.4厘米
　1984年征集
Bronze mirror with gods and animals design　Wu, Three Kingdoms Period
Diameter12.4cm　Height0.4cm
Collected in 1984
扁圆纽，圆纽座，纽座外饰二神四兽，二神呈对置式，其间四兽分成两
组，一组两兽，神兽外侧有八个方格和八个半圆相间环绕。方格上的铭
文："吾作明镜，幽湅三商。"再外为一圈锯齿纹。外区为一圈铭文带，
铭文为："五凤二年正月二十九董霸作镜。四夷服，天下太平，五谷熟，
服（著）？延寿万年。"

青铜水注 三国·吴 高8.3厘米 腹径7.9厘米
1984年马鞍山雨山区朱然墓出土
Bronze water dropper Wu,Three Kingdoms Period
Height8.3cm Globular belly diameter7.9cm
Unearthed in 1984 from Zhu Ran Tomb at Yushan
district, Ma'anshan

黑褐色，有锈斑。小口撇沿、短颈、扁圆腹。中空，可注水。有盖，纽呈蒜瓣形，盖内接吸水管，上下贯通。腹中部对称焊三个小圆管，腹下三矮蹄足。肩、腹部饰弦纹。

青铜鸡首锥盉 三国·吴 高14.6厘米 腹径14.8厘米
1984年马鞍山雨山区朱然墓出土
Bronze He-tripod with chicken-head Wu,Three Kingdoms Period
Height14.6cm Globular belly diameter14.8cm
Unearthed in 1984 from Zhu Ran Tomb at Yushan district, Ma'anshan
青灰色，器身扁圆。盖顶部有一环纽。盖与器身之间有绞链相接，
可开合。肩部鸡首伸展突出，直颈高冠，圆眼外突，为圆孔状流口，
流与腹腔相通。錾有方鋬，腹部饰弦纹，下设三瘦蹄足。

错金银青铜带钩　三国·吴　长16.0厘米
1993马鞍山金家庄区东吴墓出土
Bronze belt hook with gold-silver inlay of inscription
Wu, Three Kingdoms Period
Length16.0cm
Unearthed in 1993 from an Eastern Wu Dynasty Tomb at
Jinjiazhuang district, Ma'anshan

带钩体修长呈"S"形，钩身铸出浮雕式的兽形和长尾鸟，钩身前端作雁首形，颈部内收，从侧面看形似一曲颈昂首的鸿雁。口、眼等细部，都錾饰小点，突出轮廓。钩身铸出浮雕兽形，怀抱一条鱼，鱼鳞、鱼鳃都用阳线细刻，形态逼真，兽、鱼身上皆有滴水状的小孔，用于镶嵌松石等饰品，绿松石已失落。尾部作分歧状的尾形，点缀鸟体。钩身正面刻有"丙午钩，口含珠；手抱鱼，大吉。"错金字非常精细，圆形纽上阳刻如意花纹。

青铜弩机　三国·吴　郭长19.4厘米　望山长10.9厘米
悬刀长10.5厘米　栓塞长8.5厘米
牙板高1.1厘米　宽1.0厘米
1996年2月马鞍山东苑小区东吴墓出土
Bronze crossbow　Wu,Three Kingdoms Period
Length of guo (housing)19.4cm
Length of wangshan (a device similar to front sight of a gun)10.9cm
Length of xuandao (trigger,lit.,hanging knife)10.5cm
Unearthed in February, 1996 from an Eastern Wu tomb at Dongyuan
residential area, Ma'anshan
青铜质。郭面有矢道、弩牙、望山，望山与郭面成90度夹角。栓塞
帽头六瓣形，缺一栓塞。弩机悬刀上有铭文"右将军士俞□弩"。

青铜熨斗　三国·吴　高4.5厘米　口径8.3厘米　柄长22.0厘米
1984年马鞍山雨山区朱然墓出土
Bronze iron　Wu,Three Kingdoms Period
Height4.5cm　Mouth diameter8.3cm　Handle length22.0cm
Unearthed in 1984 from Zhu Ran Tomb at Yushan district, Ma'anshan
青铜质。宽折沿，浅腹，底微圈，柄截面为半圆形。

吳故夷道督奮威將軍諸暨都卿侯會稽孟潑息男壹為斌買
子周壽所有丹楊蕪湖馬頭山冢地一丘東出大道西極山南北左右各廣
五十丈直錢五十萬即日交畢關連橋刺蘇齊謹破券以解是為明

鳳皇三年八月十九日對共破券

锡地券 三国·吴　长36.8厘米 宽4.3厘米
马鞍山当涂县龙山桥乡东吴墓出土
Land deed in tin　Wu, Three Kingdoms Period
Length36.8cm　Breadth4.3cm
Unearthed from an Eastern Wu Dynasty tomb at Longshanqiao
countryside of Dangtu country, Ma'anshan
锡质。呈扁条形。券文三行九十一字。录文如下："吴故夷道督奋威将军诸暨都卿侯会稽孟潑。息男壹为诱买男子周寿所有丹杨芜湖马头山冢地一丘，东出大道，西极山，南北左右各广五十丈，直钱五十万，即日交毕。关连桥刺奸，齐谨破券，以解是为明。凤皇三年八月十九日对共破券"。

七乳青铜镜 西晋　直径16.2厘米　缘厚0.4厘米
纽径1.9厘米
马鞍山霍里镇晋墓出土
Bronze seven-nippled mirror Western Jin Dynasty
Diameter16.2cm　Height0.4cm Knob diameter
1.9cm
Unearthed from a Western Jin tonb at Huoli
town, Ma'anshan
半圆纽，圆座，纽座外内区有两圈乳钉纹。内
圈有九个小乳钉，外圈饰七只大乳钉，内外圈
之间饰卷草纹、磨齿纹，外圈乳钉之间饰青
龙、白虎、朱雀、玄武，镜平缘，饰锯齿纹、
卷草纹。

柿蒂八凤青铜镜 西晋 直径21.0厘米
纽径5.3厘米 缘厚0.4厘米
1984年征集
Bronze mirror with eight phoenixes
design Western Jin Dynasty
Diameter 21.0cm Knob diameter 5.3cm
Height 0.4cm
Collected in 1984
圆形。扁平圆纽，圆纽座。主纹有四柿蒂形
叶伸向镜缘，叶内有神树、凤鸟、蟾蜍。两
叶之间是一对凤鸟，两两相对，振翅欲飞，
近缘处是十六个连弧半圆，半圆内有珍禽异
兽。素缘。

六面青铜印　东晋　高3.2厘米　纽高1.0厘米
1984年11月马鞍山谢沈墓出土
Bronze seal carved on six sides
Eastern Jin Dynasty
Height3.2cm　Knob height1.0cm
Unearthed in 1984 from XieShen Tomb,
Ma'anshan
纽上有一圆孔，纽顶端和印底有阴文，纽
顶为"白记"，印底为"谢沈"，四面分
别为"臣沈"、"谢沈白笺"、"谢沈白
事"、"谢文仲"等内容。

青铜唾壶　东晋　高11.0厘米　口径10.0厘米
底径10.2厘米
1984年马鞍山雨山乡征集
Bronze spittoon　Eastern Jin Dynasty
Height11.0cm　Mouth diameter10.0cm
Base diameter 10.2cm
Collected in 1984 from Yushan countryside,
 Ma'anshan
浅盘口，扁圆腹，假圈足。

青铜博山炉　东晋　高15.1厘米　底径11.0厘米
1992年5月马鞍山慈湖乡晋墓出土
Bronze BoShan incense burner　Eastern Jin Dynasty
Height15.1cm　Base diameter 11.0cm
Unearthed in May,1992 from an Eastern Jin tomb at Cihu countryside, Ma'anshan
青铜质。上有盖，盖高而尖并雕镂成山峦形，象征着海上仙山"博山"，一侧
有开启的纽。上有镂孔，刻划三角形几何纹，竹节形承柱，下有底盘，盘口外侈。

海狮葡萄青铜镜 唐 直径10.0厘米 纽径1.4厘米
1980年9月征集
Bronze mirror with grape and sea-lion design Tang Dynasty
Diameter10.0cm Knob diameter1.4cm
Collected in September, 1980
圆形。兽纽，背面纹饰为浮雕海狮葡萄，以双线将镜背分成内外区，
内区饰四只不同姿势的海狮，与葡萄枝叶浑然一体。外区两串葡萄与
三只海狮，六只鸟雀组成一周纹带。

青铜权 元 通高16.1厘米 底径8.0厘米
1999年马鞍山当涂城关镇征集
Bronze Quan-weight Yuan Dynasty
Height 16.1cm Breadth8.0cm Base diameter8.0cm
Collected in 1999 from Chengguan town of Dangtu country
元宝式纽。上部宝柱形，下部三层圆台形，阳刻文
字"太平路"、"天六"、"泰定四年"（1327）。

马鞍山文物聚珍

漆木器

LACQUER WARES

TREASURE COLLECTION OF CULTURAL
RELICS OF MA'ANSHAN

◎

第三部分

贵族生活图漆盘　三国·吴　盘径24.8厘米
1984年马鞍山雨山区朱然墓出土
Painted lacquer dish　Wu,Three Kingdoms Period
Dish diameter24.8cm
Unearthed in 1984 from Zhu Ran Tomb at Yushan district, Ma'anshan

木胎。平沿直口，浅腹平底，沿与腹下各有一道鎏金铜。盘内壁及底髹
红漆，外壁及底髹黑红漆。盘内绘十二人，分为三层。上层为宴宾图，
画面五人。中间一豆形器，内有一勺。左边一男一女当是主人，一侍女
立于一旁，右边是两男宾。宾主都坐在圆形座垫上，似正畅谈。座前有
矮足圆盘，上放食物。中层也绘五人。左边是梳妆图，画中一女子坐在
镜架前梳妆，旁置一奁，盖已揭开。中间画对弈图，两男子分坐两边，
中间置一棋盘，前有矮足圆盘，上置食物。右边画驯鹰图，两人对坐，
手背前举，各架一鹰，中间置矮足圆盘，上置食物。下层似为出游图，
画面二人，一人骑马，一人跟于马后，前后有山岳。

童子对棍图漆盘　三国·吴　盘径14.0厘米
1984年马鞍山雨山区朱然墓出土
Painted lacquer dish　Wu, Three Kingdoms Period
Dish diameter14.0cm
Unearthed in 1984 from Zhu Ran Tomb at Yushan district, Ma'anshan
木胎。敞口，浅腹，腹底交界处有一凸弦纹。外壁及底髹黑红漆，底部用朱红漆书"蜀郡作牢"四字铭。盘内外圈黑红漆地上饰云龙纹。向内一圈红漆地上饰鱼、莲蓬、水波纹。盘中心黑红漆地上部画山峰，山前空地上有两童子持棍对舞。

季札挂剑图漆盘 三国·吴 盘径24.8厘米
1984年马鞍山雨山区朱然墓出土
Painted lacquer dish Wu,Three Kingdoms Period
Dish diameter24.8cm
Unearthed in 1984 from Zhu Ran Tomb at Yushan district, Ma'anshan
木胎。敞口，浅腹，腹底交界处有一道凸弦纹，边缘鎏金铜扣。盘背面髹黑红漆。底部用朱红漆书"蜀郡造作牢"五字铭，字体在篆隶之间。盘内外圈黑红漆地上绘狩猎纹。向内一圈红漆地上绘莲蓬、鲤鱼、鳜鱼、白鹭啄鱼、童子戏鱼等图案。盘中心绘春秋时期吴公子"季札挂剑，徐君冢树"的历史故事，歌颂了君子恪守信义的高尚情操。

宫闱宴乐图漆案　三国·吴　高3.8厘米　长82.0厘米　宽56.5厘米
1984年马鞍山雨山区朱然墓出土
Painted lacquer narrow table　Wu, Three Kingdoms Period
Height3.8cm　Length82.0cm　Breadth56.5cm
Unearthed in 1984 from Zhu Ran Tomb at Yushan district, Ma'anshan

木胎，髹黑中偏红漆地。案面长方形，缘略高，四角及边缘间隔镶有鎏金铜皮。案背附两木托，托两端有孔，可安放矮足，足已残。正面主体图案为宫闱宴乐场面。绘五十五个人物，大都附有榜题。上排左起帷帐中皇帝、嫔妃并坐、宫女侍立；其右依次为皇后、子本、平乐侯及夫人、都亭侯及夫人、长沙侯及夫人等跽坐于席上。席前置矮足圆盘，盘中盛食物；下方左起绘虎贲持钺、黄门侍郎举案、侍者恭立。中下排大部分为百戏场面，有弄丸、弄剑、武女、寻橦、连倒、转车轮等节目，还有鼓吹伴奏者。此外，上部窗外绘数人观望；左下角绘"大官门"、值门人、女值使和"大官食具"；右下角是羽林郎持弓守立。漆案主体图案四周由内及外共有五层纹饰带，髹黑红、灰、褐、赭等漆色，绘云气、禽兽、菱形、蔓草等纹饰。案背髹黑红漆，周缘饰点碎纹，正中用朱红漆篆书"官"字铭。

073

马鞍山文物聚珍 **漆 木 器**

犀皮黄口羽觞 三国·吴 高2.4厘米 长9.6厘米 宽5.6厘米
1984年马鞍山雨山区朱然墓出土
Lacquer elliptical cup Wu,Three Kingdoms Period
Height2.4cm Length9.6cm Breadth5.6cm
Unearthed in 1984 from Zhu Ran Tomb at Yushan district, Ma'anshan
皮胎。椭圆口，平底，月牙形耳。耳及口沿镶鎏金铜扣，器身装饰
属"黑面红中黄底片云纹犀皮"工艺。器表光滑，正面黑色，花纹
不显著；背面黑、红、黄色相间，花纹回转流畅富于变化。

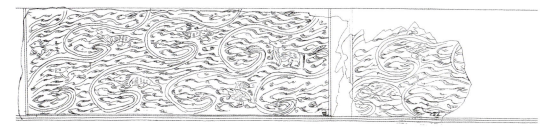

锥刻戗金漆方盒盖　三国·吴　高11.5厘米　边长22.6厘米
1984年马鞍山雨山区朱然墓出土
Lacquer rectangular box cover　Wu,Three Kingdoms Period
Height11.5cm　Side22.6cm×22.6cm
Unearthed in 1984 from Zhu Ran Tomb at Yushan　district, Ma'anshan

木胎。盒盖平面呈正方形，转角圆缓。顶面和盒四侧面针刻青龙、白虎、朱雀、麒麟、元禄等带翅神禽神兽六十五个，神禽神兽间用云纹相贯联。其中最精彩的是两面所刻的三个人物：一人右佩剑，拱手而立；一留胡须者持节行走；另一人双手拥旗而立。三人周围云气萦绕。线条简洁流畅，人物神态逼真，刻纹内戗金。

漆槅　三国·吴　高4.9厘米　长25.4厘米　宽16.3厘米
1984年马鞍山雨山区朱然墓出土
Lacquer food tray　Wu, Three Kingdoms Period
Height4.9cm　Length25.4cm　Breadth16.3cm
Unearthed in 1984 from Zhu Ran Tomb at Yushan district, Ma'anshan

木胎。槅呈长方形，子口，壶门形足。四壁外侧及底部髹黑红漆，绘蔓草纹和放鹰图。内分为七格，分别绘神禽或神兽。上排三格，中间一格较大，格内绘两凤鸟相对，曲颈挺胸，展翅振尾，翩翩起舞；左边格内绘一只天鹿，生双翅，四蹄飞扬；右边格内绘一飞鱼，鲤鱼鸡足，脊生双翼，欲展翅腾飞。下排四格，左右两格较大，中间两格较小。左格内绘麒麟，身似鹿，独角，背生双翅，牛尾，蹄足，肃立；右格内绘白虎，双翼，长尾，作奔跑状；中间左小格内绘飞廉，鹿首，双翅，双足，蛇尾；中间右小格内绘双鱼并行，其状如鲤。

武帝生活图漆盘　三国·吴　直径10.2厘米
1984年马鞍山雨山区朱然墓出土
Painted lacquer dish　Wu, Three Kingdoms Period
Dish diameter10.2cm
Unearthed in 1984 from Zhu Ran Tomb at Yushan district, Ma'anshan
木胎。盘中心绘五个人物，上部二人，下部三人。左上一人跪行，展
开双臂，作舞蹈状，右书"相夫人"三字。右上一人，注视对方，前
书"武帝"二字，二人间置杯盘和一棋盘。左下一人，回首仰视，两
臂前后舞动，左书"王女也"。下部中间一人跪坐状，前书"丞相也"
三字。下右一人跪坐状，前书"侍郎"二字。盘底黑漆以细线条勾勒
连云纹。

漆匕 三国·吴 长12.4厘米 宽4.1厘米 厚0.8厘米
1984年马鞍山雨山区朱然墓出土
Painted lacquer Bi   Wu, Three Kingdoms Period
Length12.4cm   Breadth4.1cm   Height 0.8cm
Unearthed in 1984 from Zhu Ran Tomb at Yushan district, Ma'anshan

木胎。呈长舌形。黑红漆地上用红、金两色在匕两面绘出不同的装饰图案，图案均分上中下三层，由两组上下对应的单层羽纹和窄条网纹分隔。以左边上下图（正背面）这件漆匕为例：一面上部绘凤，中部绘卷云纹，下部绘双头蛇；另一面上部绘一凤鸟，中部绘卷云纹，下部绘一龙。主体纹周围满饰云纹。

木 刺 三国·吴 长24.8厘米 宽3.4厘米 厚0.6厘米
1984年马鞍山雨山区朱然墓出土
Wooded Ci-card Wu,Three Kingdoms Period
Length24.8cm Breadth3.4cm Height0.6cm
Unearthed in 1984 from Zhu Ran Tomb at Yushan district,
Ma'anshan

木质。呈长条形。这组木刺形制大小相同，正面直行墨书，字体隶中带楷。木刺行文依次为：
"弟子朱然再拜问起居字义封"。
"故鄣朱然再拜问起居字义封"。
"丹杨朱然再拜问起居故鄣字义封"。

马鞍山文物聚珍

陶瓷器

POTTERY AND
PORCELAIN WARES

TREASURE COLLECTION OF CULTURAL
RELICS OF MA'ANSHAN

◎ 第四部分

印纹硬陶罐　西周　高13.0厘米　口径12.0厘米　底径13.0厘米
1987年马鞍山当涂县博望镇西周墓出土
Pottery jar with impressed checked design　Western Zhou Dynasty
Height13.0cm　Mouth diameter12.0cm　Base diameter13.0cm
Unearthed in1987 from a Western Zhou Dynasty tomb at Bowang
town of Dangtu county, Ma'anshan
印纹陶。子母口，鼓腹，底内凹，腹部饰方格纹不及底。

陶 罐 西周 高15.5厘米 口径14.0厘米 底径9.6厘米
2002年马鞍山霍里镇五担岗遗址出土
Pottery jar   Western Zhou Dynasty
Height15.5cm   Mouth diameter14.0cm   Base diameter9.6cm
Unearthed in 2002 from Wudangang site at Huoli town, Ma'anshan
泥质灰陶。侈口，圆唇，折肩，弧腹，平底。肩部有二道凹弦纹，
腹部饰绳纹。

陶双系罐 西周 高23.7厘米 口径16.3厘米 底径14.5厘米
2002年马鞍山霍里镇五担岗遗址出土
Pottery jar with two loop handle rings   Western Zhou Dynasty
Height23.7cm   Mouth diameter16.3cm   Base diameter14.5cm
Unearthed in 2002 from Wudangang site at Huoli town, Ma'anshan
泥质灰陶。敛口，折沿，溜肩，鼓腹，平底。肩置一对耳，器身饰
绳纹。

陶甑 西周 高18.8厘米 口径23.6厘米 底径14.0厘米
2002年马鞍山霍里镇五担岗遗址出土
Pottery Zeng-pot   Western Zhou Dynasty
Height18.8cm   Mouth diameter23.6cm   Base diameter14.0cm
Unearthed in 2002 from Wudangang site at Huoli town, Ma'anshan
泥质红陶。敛口，圆唇，深弧腹，平底。肩置一对系，器身饰绳纹，底部有镂孔。

陶豆 西周 高22.0厘米 口径23.0厘米
2002年马鞍山霍里镇五担岗遗址出土
Pottery Dou stemmed vessel   Western Zhou Dynasty
Height22.0cm   Mouth diameter23.0cm
Unearthed in 2002 from Wudangang site at Huoli town, Ma'anshan
泥质红陶。浅盘口，高喇叭状豆柄，胎质细腻，胎壁较薄，通体素面，显得素淡清雅。

陶鼎 西周 高16.0厘米 口径21.0厘米
2002年马鞍山霍里镇五担岗遗址出土
Pottery Ding-tripod   Western Zhou Dynasty
Height16.0cm   Mouth diameter21.0cm
Unearthed in 2002 from Wudangang site at Huoli town, Ma'anshan
夹砂红陶。多口，圆唇，扁圆腹，底部较平，下承以三足，足跟略外撇，显得敦实平稳。器身拍印绳纹。

陶鬲 西周 高27.0厘米 口径26.0厘米
2002年马鞍山霍里镇五担岗遗址出土
Pottery Li-vessel   Wu, Three Kingdoms Period
Height27.0cm   Mouth diameter26.0cm
Unearthed in 2002 from Wudangang site at Huoli town, Ma'anshan
夹砂黑陶。敛口，斜折沿，深腹略鼓，三足较长，足跟为柱状。通体拍印绳纹，纹饰深而清晰。

陶 瓿 西汉 高31.5厘米 口径14.5厘米 底径16.4厘米
2002年6月征集
Pottery Bu-pot Western Han Dynasty
Height31.5cm Mouth diameter14.5cm Base diameter16.4cm
Collected in June, 2002
胎灰中泛红，腹部以上饰青黄釉。直口，平沿，溜肩，弧腹，
平底。肩对称竖置一对蕉叶形系，系上贴横"8"形泥条。

陶瓿 汉 高18.0厘米 口径9.0厘米
2002年6月征集
Pottery Bu-pot Western Han Dynasty
Height18.0cm Mouth diameter9.0cm
Collected in June, 2002
胎灰中泛红，青黄釉不及底。直口，平沿，溜肩，弧腹，平底内凹。
肩部施二组凹弦纹，对称竖置一对铺首。

马鞍山文物聚珍│陶瓷器

青瓷磨 三国·吴 高5.3厘米 口径13.5厘米 底径7.1厘米
1983年2月马鞍山佳山乡东吴墓出土
Celadon mill　Wu, Three Kingdoms Period
Height5.3cm　Mouth diameter13.5cm　Base diameter7.1cm
Unearthed in February, 1983 from an Eastern Wu Dynasty tomb at Jiashan
countryside, Ma'anshan
灰白胎，淡青釉。磨模型，分为上下两扇，上扇中部为两个相对的深
槽，下扇表面刻有辐射状的沟槽。

陶 灶 三国·吴 高15.2厘米 长28.0厘米 宽22.0厘米
2005年马鞍山雨山区东吴墓出土
Pottery stove　Wu, Three Kingdoms Period
Height15.2cm　Length28.0cm　Breadth22.0cm
Unearthed in 2005 from an Eastern Wu Dynasty tomb at Yushan district,
Ma'anshan
泥质灰陶。整体呈船形，台面前高后低，双灶眼，上置两釜一甑，
前有火眼，后有火门。

陶厕圈　三国·吴　高20.2厘米　长37.5厘米
1998年7月马鞍山金家庄区寺门口东吴墓出土
Pottery hog pen　Wu, Three Kingdoms Period
Height20.2cm　Length37.5cm
Unearthed in July, 1998 from Simenkou Tomb of Eastern Wu Dynasty at
Jinjiazhuang district, Ma'anshan
泥质灰陶。圈近似正方形，四周有围墙，墙头有瓦棱。圈中有方形
厕，厕为歇山顶。栏墙处有一上坡道，通往厕门。圈内立有一头猪，
体硕大，张口竖耳。另有一戴帽陶俑，面相丑陋，呈匍匐状。

釉陶囷　三国·吴
高11.5～10.9厘米　宽12.0～13.3厘米　底径10.0～10.2厘米
1983年2月马鞍山佳山乡东吴墓出土
Pottery barns　Wu, Three Kingdoms Period
Height11.5～10.9cm　Breadth12.0～13.3cm
Base diameter10.0～10.2cm
Unearthed in Febrary, 1983 from an Eastern Wu Dynasty tomb at
Jiashan countryside, Ma'anshan
The other: Height10.9cm　Breadth13.3cm　Base diameter10.2 cm
两件。胎灰中略泛红，褐色釉不及底，攒尖顶，囷身开一小门。

釉陶囷　三国·吴　高15.0厘米　腹径12.3厘米
1984年6月马鞍山雨山区朱然墓出土
Glazed pottery barns　Wu, Three Kingdoms Period
Height15.0cm　Globular belly diameter12.3cm
Unearthed in June, 1984 from Zhu Ran Tomb at Yushan district,
Ma'anshan
两件。灰白胎，褐黄釉不及底。攒尖顶，饰瓦棱纹，附加三泥条脊，
左边囷身饰两道弦纹，右边囷身饰水波纹，弦纹之间开一小门。

釉陶跽坐俑 三国·吴 高17.0~16.3厘米
1983年2月马鞍山佳山乡东吴墓出土
Glazed Pottery figurine of a crouches man with his slightly parted lips
Wu, Three Kingdoms Period
Height17.0~16.3cm
Unearthed in Febrary, 1983 from an Eastern Wu Dynasty tomb at Jiashan
countryside, Ma'anshan
两件。灰胎，青绿釉。二俑均呈跽坐姿态，双手合于胸前。一头扎方
巾，一面部丰满，肥鼻大眼，头戴尖顶帽，前额有凸起的"白毫"。

釉陶钱纹罐 三国·吴 通高31.3厘米 口径19.6厘米 底径15.8厘米
1984年6月马鞍山雨山区朱然墓出土
Glazed pottery jar with coin design　Wu, Three Kingdoms Period
Total height31.3cm　Mouth diametercm19.6cm　Base diameter15.8cm
Unearthed in June, 1984 from Zhu Ran Tomb at Yushan district, Ma'anshan
灰白胎，黄褐釉不及底。方唇，口微侈，短直颈，丰肩，鼓腹，腹下
部内收，小平底。颈部、肩部饰弦纹，由肩及上腹部拍印钱纹，下腹
部拍印几何纹。

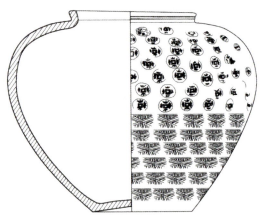

青瓷鸡首罐 三国·吴 高19.2厘米 口径10.5厘米
1987年10月马鞍山雨山乡宋山东吴墓出土
Celadon jar with chicken-head Wu, Three Kingdoms Period
Height19.2cm Mouth diameter10.5cm
Unearthed in October, 1987 from Songshan Tomb of Eastern Wu Dynasty
at Yushan countryside, Ma'anshan
灰白胎，青釉。方唇，短直颈，溜肩，鼓腹，平底内凹。颈、肩部饰
四道弦纹。肩置两对半环形耳，耳上饰蕉叶纹，两耳中间置有颈鸡
首，鸡嘴与腹相通，微张，对称处有一上翘鸡尾。

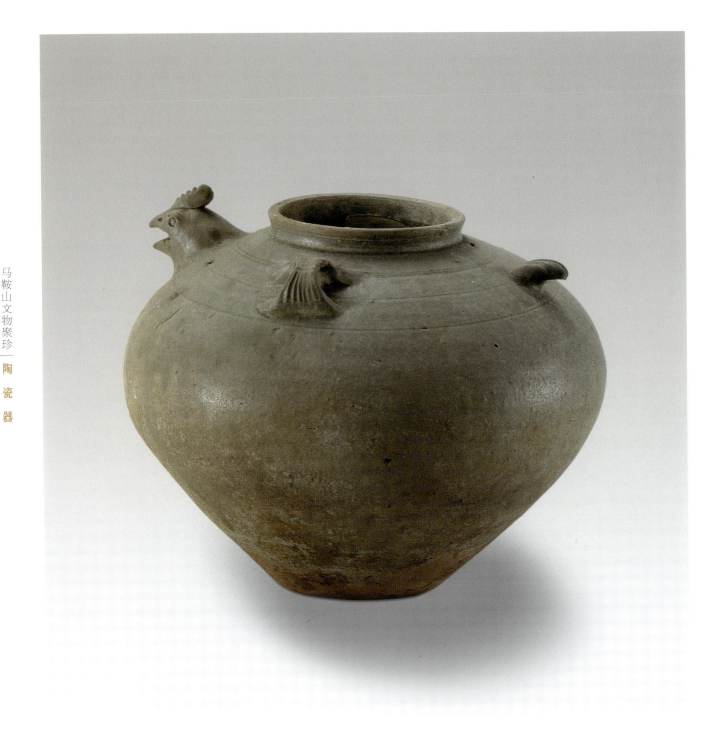

青瓷鸡首罐 三国·吴 高19.2厘米 口径10.5厘米
1987年10月马鞍山雨山乡宋山东吴墓出土
Celadon jar withchicken-head Wu, Three Kingdoms Period
Height19.2cm Mouth diameter10.5cm
Unearthed in October, 1987 from Songshan Tomb of Eastern Wu Dynasty
at Yushan countryside, Ma'anshan
灰白胎，豆青釉不及底。方唇，短直颈，溜肩鼓腹，平底内凹。颈、
肩部饰六道弦纹。肩置两对称半环形耳，耳上饰蕉叶纹，两耳中间置
无颈鸡首，鸡嘴与腹相通，微张，对称处置有一鸡尾，尾尖略下垂。

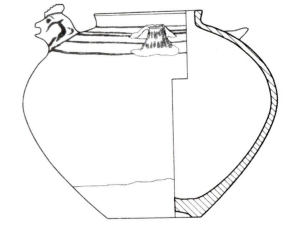

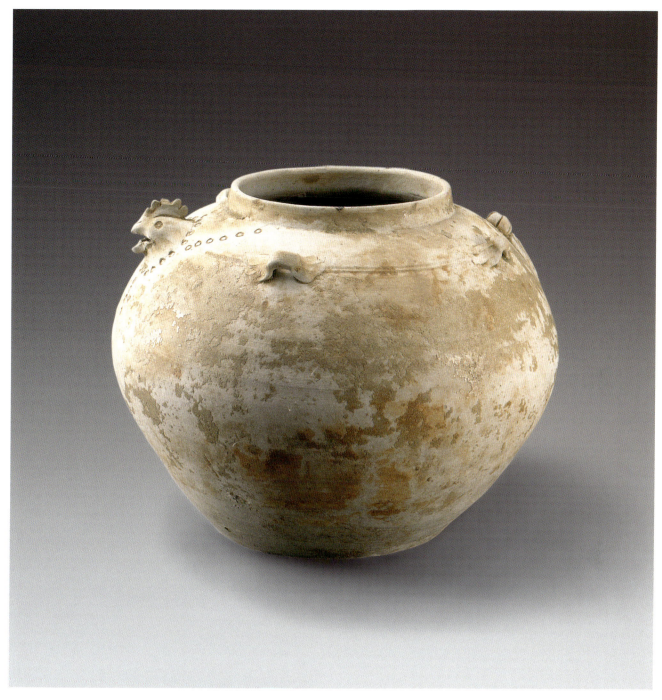

青瓷鸡首罐 三国·吴 高20.8厘米 口径13.3厘米 底径15.2厘米
1998年7月马鞍山金家庄区寺门口东吴墓出土
Celadon jar with chicken-head Wu, Three Kingdoms Period
Height20.8cm Mouth diameter13.3cm Base diameter15.2cm
Unearthed in July, 1998 from Simenkou Tomb of Eastern Wu Dynasty at
Jinjiazhuang district, Ma'anshan
灰白胎，淡青釉不及底。方唇，短直颈，溜肩，鼓腹，平底。肩部饰
两道凹弦纹。肩横置四个蟹爪系，鸡首无颈，鸡首四周饰联珠纹，鸡
嘴与腹相通，鸡首对称处堆贴一花瓣结绳纹尾，鸡尾紧贴腹部。

青瓷兽首罐　三国·吴　高23.3厘米　口径12.0厘米　底径11.0厘米
1975年马鞍山当涂县太白乡东吴墓出土
Celadon jar with animal-head　Wu, Three Kingdoms Period
Height23.3cm　Mouth diameter12.0cm　Base diameter11.0cm
Unearthed in 1975 from an Eastern Wu Dynasty tomb at Taibai countryside
of Dangtu country, Ma'anshan
灰白胎，豆青釉不及底。蒜瓣纽盖。圆唇，溜肩，鼓腹，底内凹。盖
上饰五道凹弦纹，上腹部有对称蕉叶纹双耳，两耳之间饰一兽首，张
嘴，对称处堆贴一兽尾。

青瓷水盂　三国·吴　高3.4厘米　口径3.6厘米　底径3.8厘米
2005年马鞍山雨山区东吴墓出土
Celadon water container　Wu, Three Kingdoms Period
Height3.4cm　Mouth diameter3.6cm　Base diameter3.8cm
Unearthed in 2005 from an Eastern Wu Dynasty tomb at Yushan
district, Ma'anshan
灰白胎，豆青釉。敛口，丰肩，扁圆腹，平底略凹，近底处
刻划一道凹弦纹。

青瓷束口罐　三国·吴　高21.0厘米　口径9.4厘米　底径9.5厘米
1987年10月马鞍山雨山乡宋山东吴墓出土
Celadon jar contracted mouth　Wu, Three Kingdoms Period
Height21.0cm　Mouth diameter9.4cm　Base diameter9.5cm
Unearthed in October, 1987 from Songshan Tomb of Eastern Wu Dynasty at
Yushan countryside, Ma'anshan
灰白胎，豆青釉。直筒状，方唇，短直颈，方折肩，平底内凹。

青瓷双系罐 三国·吴 高11.8厘米 口径8.2厘米
1987年10月马鞍山雨山乡宋山东吴墓出土
Celadon jar with two loop handle rings Wu, Three Kingdoms Period
Height11.8cm Mouth diameter8.2cm
Unearthed in October, 1987 from Songshan Tomb of Eastern Wu Dynasty
at Yushan countryside, Ma'anshan
灰白胎，青灰釉不及底。圆唇，短直颈，鼓腹内敛，平底内凹。肩部
饰有三道凹弦纹，对称处置两泥条系。

青瓷四系罐 三国·吴 高15.0厘米 口径14.0厘米 底径9.0厘米
1987年10月马鞍山雨山乡宋山东吴墓出土
Celadon jar with four loop handle rings Wu, Three Kingdoms Period
Height15.0cm Mouth diameter14.0cm Base diameter9.0cm
Unearthed in October, 1987 from Songshan Tomb of Eastern Wu Dynasty
at Yushan countryside, Ma'anshan
灰白胎，青灰釉不及底。圆唇，侈口，鼓腹内敛，底内凹。肩部饰
有三道凹弦纹，对称横置四个兽爪形系。

青瓷卣形壶　三国·吴　高22.3厘米　口径11.4厘米×10.3厘米
底径12.8厘米
1996年6月马鞍山雨山区朱然墓出土
Celadon You-vessel　Wu, Three Kingdoms Period
Height22.3cm　Mouth diameter11.4cm×10.3cm　Base diameter12.8cm
Unearthed in June, 1996 from Zhu Ran Tomb at Yushan district, Ma'anshan
灰白胎，蟹壳青釉。椭圆口，短直颈，椭圆腹，圈足外撇，器底内凹。
肩部压印联珠纹、菱形网格纹及锯齿纹，每组纹饰以弦纹相隔；圈足两
道弦纹之间饰菱形网格纹。肩部四周对称贴塑四个羊形铺首，长径方向
的一对铺首较大，上附泥条形耳；短径方向的一对铺首较小，紧贴在壶
壁上。

青瓷香熏　三国·吴　高15.9厘米　口径17.8厘米　底径13.1厘米
1984年马鞍山雨山区朱然墓出土
Celadon incense burner　Wu, Three Kingdoms Period
Height15.9cm　Mouth diameter17.8cm　Base diameter13.1cm
Unearthed in 1984 from Zhu Ran Tomb at Yushan district, Ma'anshan
灰白胎，青釉不及底。篮形，圆唇短颈，溜肩，扁圆腹，圈足外撇，
足底内部略凹。肩部饰弦纹和网格纹带，两侧置对称泥条双系。肩
腹部镂孔五排九十五个，排列略不规整。底部孔九个。所镂孔径在
1.3～1.6厘米之间，大小不等。

青瓷虎子　三国·吴　高16.2厘米　口径4.1厘米　底径12.0厘米
1995年5月马鞍山金家庄区东吴墓出土
Celadon Huzi-vessel　Wu, Three Kingdoms Period
Height16.2cm　Mouth diameter4.1cm　Base diameter12.0cm
Unearthed in May, 1995 from an Eastern Wu Dynasty tomb at Jinjiazhuang
district, Ma'anshan
灰白胎，青黄釉。口沿外撇，贴有捏塑鼻、眼、耳。圆泥条提梁，扁
圆腹，腹上有数条弦纹，平底。

青瓷虎子 三国·吴 高17.4厘米 长22.4厘米 口径6.0厘米
1996年1月马鞍山东苑小区东吴墓出土
Celadon Huzi-vessel Wu, Three Kingdoms Period
Height17.4cm Length22.4cm Mouth diameter6.0cm
Unearthed in January, 1996 from an Eastern Wu Dynasty tomb at
Dongyuan residential area, Ma'anshan
灰白胎，青灰釉。体呈蚕茧形，圆口方唇，堆塑、刻划虎头。
鼻孔上仰，双目突出，两耳上竖，耳旁有鬃毛。背上有圆形
细长提梁，提梁末端贴有细小尾。两肋刻划双翼。下有蹲伏
四足，足为五爪。

青瓷提梁虎子 三国·吴 高18.9厘米 长20.8厘米 口径4.5厘米
1998年征集
Celadon Huzi-vessel with loop handle Wu Three Kingdoms Period
Height18.9cm Length20.8cm Mouth diameter4.5cm
Collected in 1998

灰白胎，豆青釉。圆口方唇，虎头双目圆睁，双耳竖立，两肋刻划羽翼，四足呈卧状，脚趾刻划清晰，背上附一环形提梁，上刻戳刺纹。

青瓷灶 三国·吴 高12.8厘米 口径24.5厘米 底径19.0厘米
1983年2月马鞍山佳山乡东吴墓出土
Celadon stove Wu, Three Kingdoms Period
Height12.8cm Mouth diameter24.5cm Base diameter19.0cm
Unearthed in February, 1983 from an Eastern Wu Dynasty tomb at Jiashan
countryside, Ma'anshan

灰白胎，淡青釉。整体呈船形，台面前高后低，台上有两釜，前有火眼，后有火门。

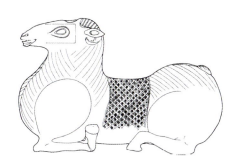

青瓷羊　三国·吴　高21.0厘米 长33.2厘米
1996年9月马鞍山雨山区朱然家族墓出土
Celadon ram-shaped holder　Wu, Three Kingdoms Period
Hight21.0cm　Length33.2cm
Unearthed in September, 1996 from Zhu Ran family tomb at Yushan district,
Ma'anshan
灰白胎，青釉。羊身躯肥壮，四足卷曲作卧伏状，昂首张口，头顶处有一
圆孔，颈部刻划线纹，腹部饰宽菱形纹带，尾部刻划斜线纹。

青瓷牛 三国·吴 高13.1厘米 长23.6厘米
1998年马鞍山当涂县护河镇东吴墓出土
Celadon ox　Wu, Three Kingdoms Period
Height13.1cm　Length23.6cm
Unearthed in 1998 from an Eastern Wu Dynasty tomb at
Dangtu country, Ma'anshan
灰白胎，淡青釉。牛作直立行走状，犄角下弯，牛眼鼓凸，牛鼻拴一
绳绕在犄角上，牛尾卷曲，牛腿粗壮有力，足部用线条刻划成蹄状。

青瓷牛车 三国·吴 高11.8厘米 长16.0厘米 宽11.5厘米
1983年2月马鞍山佳山乡东吴墓出土
Celadon ox-drawn van　Wu, Three Kingdoms Period
Height11.8cm　Length16.0cm　Breadth11.5cm
Unearthed in February, 1983 from an Eastern Wu Dynasty tomb at
Jiashan countryside, Ma'anshan
灰白胎，车身釉已剥落，牛满身施青黄釉。牛尾下垂，埋头拉车。
车为卷棚式顶，后板刻方格网纹。

青瓷配鞍马　三国·吴　高15.0厘米　长19.2厘米
1998年马鞍山雨当涂县护河镇东吴墓出土
Celadon house with saddle　Wu, Three Kingdoms Period
Height15.0cm　Length19.2cm
Unearthed in 1998 from an Eastern Wu Dynasty tomb at Huhe town of
Dangtu country, Ma'anshan
灰白胎，淡青釉剥落。马呈直立状，有缰，便于驾驭，背部配有鞍，
鞍下部刻有水波纹，鞍上部有铆钉状饰，马尾向右弯曲至臀部。

青瓷猪圈 三国·吴 高11.0厘米 长21.0厘米 宽16.0厘米
1996年9月马鞍山雨山区朱然家族墓出土
Celadon hog pen Wu, Three Kingdoms Period
Height11.0cm Length21.0cm Breadth16.0cm
Unearthed in September, 1996 from Zhu Ran family tomb at Yushan
district, Ma'anshan
灰白胎，青黄釉不及底。猪圈呈长方形，顶有瓦棱，正面有两门，侧
面各有两窗，后面三窗。猪圈内有两猪。右为母猪，左为犍猪。

青瓷鸭笼　三国·吴　高12.0厘米　长13.5厘米　宽10.5厘米
1983年2月马鞍山佳山乡东吴墓出土
Celadon duck-coop　Wu, Three Kingdoms Period
Height12.0cm　Length13.5cm　Breadth10.5cm
Unearthed in February, 1983 from an Eastern Wu Dynasty tomb at Jiashan countryside, Ma'anshan
灰白胎，青釉。鸭笼呈长方形，五脊式屋顶，正面有一个门，门两边各有两窗。三只鸭原在笼内。

青瓷鸡笼　三国·吴　高12.0厘米　长15.0厘米　宽12.7厘米
1983年2月马鞍山佳山乡东吴墓出土
Celadon hen-coop　Wu, Three Kingdoms Period
Height12.0cm　Length15.0cm　Breadth12.7cm
Unearthed in February, 1983 from an Eastern Wu Dynasty tomb at Jiashan countryside, Ma'anshan
灰白胎，青釉。鸡笼呈长方形，五脊式屋顶，正面有两门，门两边墙上有菱形网格纹，门前有两厘米宽的台阶。三只鸡原在笼内。

青瓷马圈　三国·吴　高14.3厘米　长24.5厘米　宽18.0厘米
1996年9月马鞍山雨山区朱然家族墓出土
Celadon house pen　Wu, Three Kingdoms Period
Height14.3cm　Length24.5cm　Breadth18.0cm
Unearthed in September, 1996 from Zhu Ran family tomb at Yushan district,
Ma`anshan

灰白胎，豆青釉。马圈呈长方形，屋脊略翘，屋顶饰瓦棱纹。圈体
正中开一门，侧设两喂食口，左右及后部圈墙镂雕长条形栅栏。
圈内有马两匹，体型相似，马体略丰，四肢直立，探头竖耳，眼、
鼻、嘴戳划而成。马头顶至颈背部有鬃发，马尾下垂。

青瓷 羊圈　三国·吴　高13.0厘米　长14.8厘米　宽12.4厘米
1983年2月马鞍山佳山乡东吴墓出土
Celadon sheep pen　Wu, Three Kingdoms Period
Height13.0cm　Length14.8cm　Breadth12.4cm
Unearthed in February, 1983 from an Eastern Wu Dynasty tomb at
Jiashan countryside, Ma'anshan
灰白胎，青釉。羊圈呈长方形，五脊式屋顶，正面有三个门，
三只羊原在圈内站立，面向门外。羊两耳竖立，双角卷曲。

青瓷 厕圈　三国·吴　高11.5厘米　直径11.0厘米
1983年2月马鞍山佳山乡东吴墓出土
Celadon hog pen　Wu, Three Kingdoms Period
Height11.5cm　Diameter11.0cm
Unearthed in February, 1983 from an Eastern Wu Dynasty tomb at Jiashan
countryside, Ma'anshan
灰白胎，青绿釉。厕圈呈圆盘形，内有一猪。栏墙上有一圆形厕所，
厕所为五脊式屋顶，栏墙外有一上坡道，通往厕所门，门朝里开。

青瓷厕圈　三国·吴　高11.3厘米　长22.3厘米　宽17.0厘米
1996年9月马鞍山雨山区朱然家族墓出土
Celadon hog pen　Wu, Three Kingdoms Period
Height11.3cm　Length22.3cm　Breadth17.0cm
Unearthed in September, 1996 from Zhu Ran family tomb at Yushan
district, Ma'anshan

灰白胎，青黄釉剥落。厕圈呈长方形，屋顶有瓦棱，厕分两间，正面
有两门一窗，背面四窗，两侧各有三窗。左厕宽短，中间有隔墙，靠
前面有一门相通。

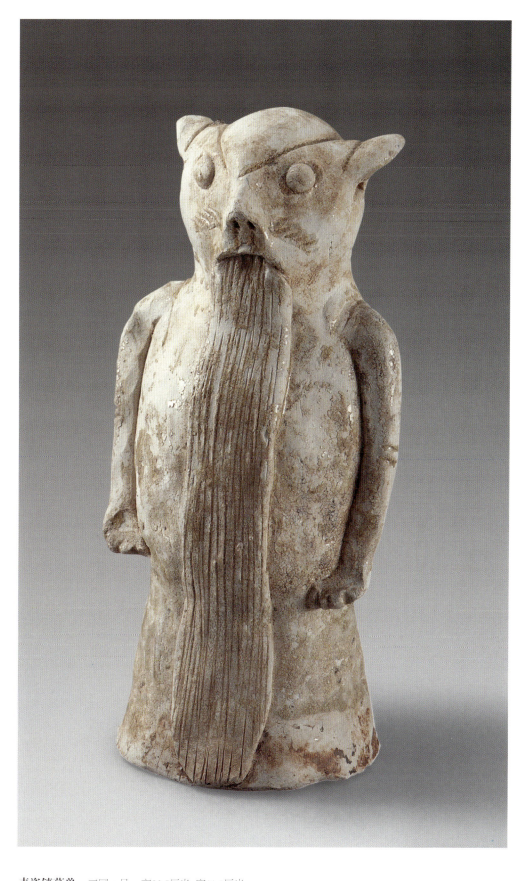

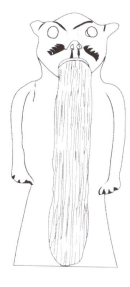

青瓷镇墓兽　三国·吴　高23.5厘米 宽11.0厘米
1996年9月马鞍山雨山区朱然家族墓出土
Celadon tomb guard　Wu, Three Kingdoms Period
Height23.5cm　Breadth11.0cm
Unearthed in September, 1996 from Zhu Ran family tomb at Yushan district, Ma'anshan
镇墓兽呈站立姿态。兽面人身，双耳竖立，双目突出，舌长及地。

青瓷镇墓兽　三国·吴　高20.4厘米　长25.0厘米
1983年2月马鞍山佳山乡东吴墓出土
Celadon tomb guard　Wu, Three Kingdoms Period
Height20.4cm　Length25.0cm
Unearthed in February, 1983 from an Eastern Wu Dynasty tomb at Jiashan countryside, Ma'anshan
灰白胎，豆青釉。人面兽身，体形肥壮。面部扁平，鼻突出，昂首竖耳，额部有一孔洞，直通下额部。

青瓷镇墓兽　三国·吴　高22.0厘米　宽23.0厘米
1998年马鞍山雨当涂县护河镇东吴墓出土
Celadon tomb guard　Wu, Three Kingdoms Period
Height22.0cm　Breadth23.0cm
Unearthed in 1998 from an Eastern Wu Dynasty tomb at Huhe town of Dangtu country, Ma'anshan
灰白胎，青釉。人面兽身，面部饱满，双目突出，舌外吐，额顶部有一犀牛角状物，体形肥壮。

陶 俑 西晋　高24.0厘米 宽9.3厘米
1990年6月马鞍山霍里镇西晋墓出土
Pottery figureine　Western Jin Dynasty
Height24.0cm　Breadth9.3cm
Unearthed in June, 1990 from a Western Jin Dynasty tomb at Huoli town,
Ma'anshan
泥质灰陶。俑面部扁平，小眼睛，高鼻梁，束发小冠，发髻插簪。上
身袒露，双手交叉于腹前，似坐于莲花形座上。

青瓷碗 西晋 高4.3厘米 口径12.0厘米
底径5.8厘米
2002年4月征集
Celadon bowl　Western Jin Dynasty
Height4.3cm　Mouth diameter12.0cm　Base
diameter5.8cm
Collected in April, 2002
灰白胎，青釉不及底。圆唇，平底内凹。唇
下有一道弦纹和一圈网格纹带，底部内外各
有四、五个支烧点。

青瓷碗 西晋 高5.2厘米 口径14.2厘米
底径7.9厘米
1986年10月马鞍山霍里镇西晋墓出土
Celadon bowl　Western Jin Dynasty
Height5.2cm　Mouth diameter14.2cm　Base
diameter7.9cm
Unearthed in October, 1986 from a Western Jin
Dynasty tomb at Huoli town, Ma'anshan
灰白胎，青釉。圆唇，平底内凹。唇下有一道
弦纹和一圈网格纹带，碗内有八个支烧点。

青瓷钵 西晋 高2.7厘米 长20.6厘米 口径10.9厘米
1996年1月马鞍山东苑小区西晋墓出土
Celadon Bo-bowl　Western Jin Dynasty
Height2.7cm　Length20.6cm　Mouth diameter10.9cm
Unearthed in January, 1996 from a Western Jin Dynasty
tomb at Dongyuan residential area, Ma'anshan
灰白胎，青釉不及底。敛口圆唇，底略呈饼形。口沿
外饰一道凹弦纹，口沿上有七处褐斑点彩。

青瓷盘口壶　西晋　高32.0厘米　口径16.6厘米　底径13.0厘米
1975年马鞍山当涂县青山乡西晋墓出土
Celadon pot with dish shaped mouth　Western Jin Dynasty
Height32.0cm　Mouth diameter16.6cm　Base diameter13.0cm
Unearthed in 1975 from a Western Jin Dynasty tomb at Qingshan
countryside of Dangtu country, Ma'anshan
灰白胎，豆青釉不及底。盘口，直颈，圆鼓腹，平底略凹。肩部有三
道弦纹，置对称双复系。

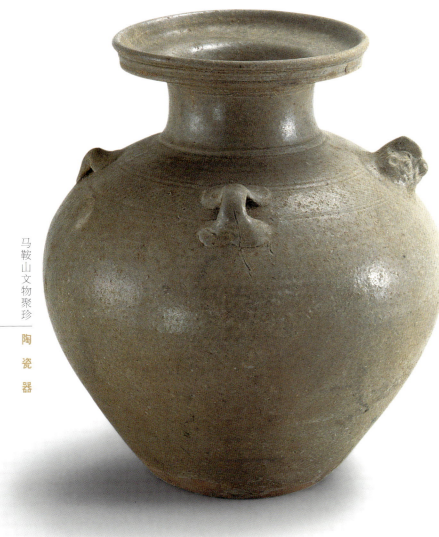

青瓷鸡首盘口壶　西晋　高18.8厘米　口径10.4厘米
底径8.0厘米
1989年4月马鞍山霍里镇征集
Celadon pot with dish-shaped mouth and chicken-
head　Western Jin Dynasty
Height18.8cm　Mouth diameter10.4cm　Base diameter8.0cm
Collected in April, 1989 at Huoli town, Ma'anshan
灰白胎，青灰釉不及底。浅盘口，溜肩，鼓腹内敛，底内
凹。口沿外侧饰一道凹弦纹，中间置两对称泥条形系，两
系间置一无颈鸡首，尖嘴无孔，对称处贴一短尾。

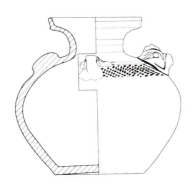

青瓷鸡首盘口壶　西晋　高8.7厘米　口径5.5厘米
底径5.2厘米
1988年5月马鞍山佳山乡西晋墓出土
Celadon pot with dish-shaped mouth and chicken-
head　Western Jin Dynasty
Height8.7cm　Mouth diameter5.5cm　Base diameter5.2cm
Unearthed in May, 1988 from a Western Jin Dynasty tomb at
Jiashan countryside, Ma'anshan
灰白胎，豆青釉不及底。浅盘口，溜肩，扁圆腹，平底内
凹。肩上饰两道凹弦纹，弦纹下饰一圈网带，网纹上置两
对称泥条形系，两系之间置一鸡首，尖嘴无孔，对称处贴
一短尾。

青瓷双系盘口壶 西晋 高23.5厘米 口径13.5厘米 底径10.7厘米
1988年马鞍山霍里镇西晋墓出土
Celadon pot with dish-shaped mouth and two loop handle rings Western Jin Dynasty
Height23.5cm Mouth diameter13.5cm Base diameter10.7cm
Unearthed in 1988 from a Western Jin Dynasty tomb at Huoli town, Ma'anshan

灰白胎，豆青釉不及底。浅盘口，短直颈，鼓腹内敛，底内凹，肩部饰三道凹弦纹，上两道弦纹间饰一圈联珠纹，下两道弦纹间饰一圈网格纹。弦纹下又饰一圈联珠纹。弦纹间等距离置衔环铺首和两半环形系，系上饰蕉叶纹。

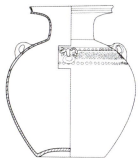

青瓷双系盘口壶 西晋 高24.9厘米 口径14.3厘米 底径10.6厘米
1984年9月马鞍山慈湖乡西晋墓出土
Celadon pot with dish-shaped mouth and two loop handle rings Western
Jin Dynasty
Height24.9cm Mouth diameter14.3cm Base diameter10.6cm
Unearthed in September, 1984 from a Western Jin Dynasty tomb at Cihu
countryside, Ma'anshan
胎中泛红，青釉不及底。浅盘口，束颈，溜肩，弧腹，平底内凹。肩
部饰一道凹弦纹，对称竖置蕉叶纹泥条系。

青瓷唾壶　西晋　高13.0厘米　口径7.5厘米　底径8.0厘米
1988年马鞍山霍里镇西晋墓出土
Celadon spittoon　Western Jin Dynasty
Height13.0cm　Mouth diameter7.5cm　Base diameter8.0cm
Unearthed in 1988 from a Western Jin Dynasty tomb at Huoli town,
Ma'anshan
灰白胎，青黄釉不及底。浅盘口，鼓腹下垂，假圈足。

青瓷双系罐 三国·吴 高6.7厘米 口径6.1厘米
底径5.0厘米
2005年马鞍山雨山区东吴墓出土
Celadon jar with two loop handle rings Wu, Three
Kingdoms Period
Height6.7cm Mouth diameter6.1cm
Base diameter5.0cm
Unearthed in 2005 from an Eastern Wu Dynasty tomb
at Yushan district, Ma'anshan
灰白胎，豆青釉。直口，圆唇，丰肩，扁圆腹，平
底略凹，肩部饰三道凹弦纹，两边对称处各竖置一
泥条系。

青瓷双系罐 西晋 高12.0厘米 口径9.8厘米
底径7.6厘米
1998年9月征集
Celadon jar with two loop handle rings Western
Jin Dynasty
Height12.0cm Mouth diameter9.8cm
Base diameter7.6cm
Collected in September, 1998
灰白胎，豆青釉。侈口，方唇，溜肩，圆鼓
腹，平底略内凹。肩部对称处各竖置一泥条
系，并饰三道弦纹和一道网格纹，底部有七个
支烧痕。

青瓷四系罐 西晋 高13.0厘米 口径10.6厘米
底径8.6厘米
1996年1月马鞍山东苑小区晋墓出土
Celadon jar with four loop handle rings
Western Jin Dynasty
Height13.0cm　Mouth diameter10.6cm
Base diameter8.6cm
Unearthed in January, 1996 from a Western Jin Dynasty
tomb at Dongyuan residential area, Ma'anshan
胎色灰中泛红，青釉不及底。侈口，圆唇，溜肩，
弧腹，平底略内凹。肩部饰三道凹弦纹，对称横置
四泥条系，底有五个支烧痕。

青瓷双复系罐 西晋 高22.0厘米 口径15.6厘米
底径12.0厘米
1987年马鞍山当涂县青山乡征集
Celadon jar with four loop handle rings
Western Jin Dynasty
Height22.0cm　Mouth diameter15.6cm
Base diameter12.0cm
Collected in 1987 at Qingshan countryside of Dangtu
county, Ma'anshan
灰白胎，豆青釉不及底。敞口，平沿，束颈，溜肩，
鼓腹下内收，平底略内凹。肩部饰两道联珠纹，其间
夹有一道网格纹。肩部对称附双蕉叶系，另有对称贴
塑"羽人骑马"图案。

青瓷鸡首四系罐 西晋 高9.3厘米 口径5.8厘米 底径7.6厘米
1998年马鞍山当涂城关镇征集
Celadon jar with chicken-head and four loop handle rings Western Jin Dynasty
Height9.3cm Mouth diameter5.8cm
Base diameter7.6cm
Collected in 1998 at Chengguan town of Dangtu country, Ma'anshan
灰白胎，豆青釉。敛口，尖唇，溜肩，鼓腹内敛，平底。肩部饰三道弦
纹，肩对称置四条形系和鸡首、鸡尾。鸡首高冠。两侧之间各贴塑一朱
雀，呈对称状。四系下各贴塑一坐佛。

青瓷奁 西晋 高7.4厘米 口径11.8厘米 底径11.5厘米
1975年马鞍山当涂县青山乡征集
Celadon Lian-toilet set　Western Jin Dynasty
Height7.4cm　Mouth diameter11.8cm　Base diameter11.5cm
Collected in 1975 at Qingshan countryside of Dangtu country,
Ma'anshan

灰白胎，青黄釉。奁呈圆筒状，方唇，平底。口沿外饰一
道凹弦纹，下饰一圈联珠纹，腹部饰两道凹弦纹，其间等
分贴塑三个衔环铺首，腹下部饰一圈网格纹。

青瓷束口罐 西晋 高18.0厘米 口径8.5厘米
底径9.7厘米
1991年7月马鞍山花山区西晋墓出土
Celadon jar contracted mouth　Western Jin Dynasty
Height18.0cm　Mouth diameter8.5cm
Base diameter9.7cm
Unearthed in July, 1991 from a Western Jin Dynasty
tomb at Huashan District, Ma'anshan

灰白胎，青黄釉不及底。罐呈喇叭形，方唇，短
直颈，方折肩，底内凹。肩上饰有网格纹和一道
凹弦纹。

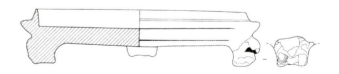

马鞍山文物聚珍 陶瓷器

青瓷三足樽 西晋 高8.5厘米 口径17.5厘米 底径9.5厘米
1988年马鞍山霍里镇西晋墓出土
Celadon Zun-cup with three legs　Western Jin Dynasty
Height8.5cm　Mouth diameter17.5cm　Base diameter9.5cm
Unearthed in 1988 from a Western Jin Dynasty tomb at Huoli town,
Ma'anshan
灰白胎，豆青釉。圆唇，口微敛，底内凹，下置三兽足。口沿
外饰四道弦纹，下两道弦纹间饰一圈网纹。网纹带上等距离置
三个衔环铺首。

青瓷三足砚 西晋 高3.7厘米 口径12.0厘米 底径11.2厘米
1990年马鞍山霍里镇西晋墓出土
Celadon inkstone with three legs　Western Jin Dynasty
Height3.7cm　Mouth diameter12.0cm　Base diameter11.2cm
Unearthed in 1990 from a Western Jin Dynasty tomb at Huoli town,
Ma'anshan
灰白胎，青黄釉。圆形，子母口，砚面不施釉，其上整齐排列六个支
烧点，砚底有三兽形足。

132

青瓷狮形插座　西晋　高11.5厘米　长16.0厘米
1986年10月马鞍山霍里镇西晋墓出土
Celadon lion-shaped holder　Western Jin Dynasty
Height11.5cm　Length16.0cm
Unearthed in October, 1986 from a Western Jin Dynasty tomb at Huoli town,
Ma'anshan
灰白胎，青釉。狮呈蹲伏状，昂首，双目突出，张口露齿，颌下有须，
尾呈蕉叶状，脊中部竖一管状插孔与腹部相通。

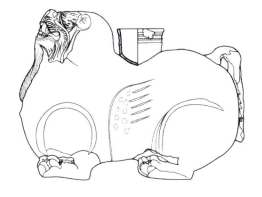

青瓷魂瓶 西晋 高40.0厘米 底径16.0厘米
1987年马鞍山当涂县太白乡西晋墓出土
Celadon funerary vase Western Jin Dynasty
Height40.0cm Base diameter16.0cm
Unearthed in 1987 from a Western Jin Dynasty
tomb at Taibai countryside of Dangtu country,
Ma'anshan

灰白胎，青黄釉。罐上部堆塑两层楼台，一层
塑双阙、门楼及10名跽坐拱手胡俑；二层为正
方形建筑，顶部作庑殿式，四周有角楼。下半
部罐体溜肩收腹，平底略凹。腹部交错附贴麒
麟、羽人骑马、游鱼等图案。

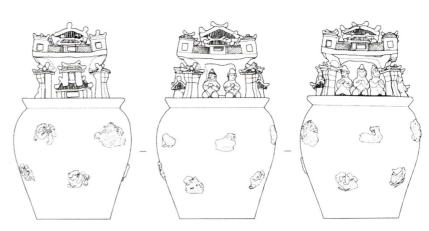

青瓷魂瓶　西晋　高42.0厘米　底径17.0厘米
1998年马鞍山当涂县太白乡西晋墓出土
Celadon funerary vase　Western Jin Dynasty
Height42.0cm　Base diameter17.0cm
Unearthed in 1998 from a Western Jin Dynasty tomb at Taibai countryside
of Dangtu country, Ma'anshan

灰白胎，豆青釉不及底。罐上堆塑三层楼阁，一层为双阙、胡僧、门
楼；二、三层为五联罐演变而来，四周众鸟簇拥。罐体溜肩，鼓腹，
腹部堆贴有螃蟹、鱼、龙、青蛙、羽人骑马、坐佛等图案，另线刻
鹤、熊等形象。

孟府君墓砖　东晋　长35.0厘米　宽17.0厘米　厚5.0厘米
1976年5月马鞍山花山区孟府君墓出土
Carved bricks of Mengfujun Tomb　Eastern Jin Dynasty
Length35.0cm　Breadth 17.0cm　Height 5.0cm
Unearthed in 1976 from Mengfujun Tomb at Huashan district, Ma'anshan
这这五块墓志铭文内容相同，书体各异。每块墓砖行文三行，共29字，
内容："泰元元年十二月十二日晋故平昌郡安丘县始兴相散骑常侍孟
府君墓"。泰元是东晋孝武帝司马曜年号，泰元元年即公元376年。
书法古朴、洒脱、超逸，隶、楷、行诸体兼而有之。

灰陶无常俑 东晋 通高17.2厘米
1979年马鞍山当涂县青山乡东晋墓出土
Grey pottery WuChang-figurine Eastern Jin Dynasty
Total height17.2cm
Unearthed in 1979 from an Eastern Jin Dynasty tomb at
Qingshan countryside of Dangtu country, Ma'anshan
泥质灰陶。俑呈跪坐姿，头戴元宝形尖角帽，眉毛微翘，
双目向前平视，鼻子尖挺，口微张，吐舌至膝部，双手交
叉置于腹部，上身挺立，两腿修长并拢跪坐。

青瓷碗 东晋 高4.2厘米 口径10.4厘米 底径5.8厘米
2001年9月马鞍山花园小区晋墓出土
Celadon bowl Eastern Jin Dynasty
Height4.2cm Mouth diameter10.4cm Base diameter5.8cm
Unearthed in September, 2001 from an Eastern Jin Dynasty
tomb at Huayuan residential area, Ma'anshan
灰白胎，青釉，釉开片。圆唇，平底内凹。唇下有一道弦
纹，底部内外各有四个支烧点。

青瓷双系盘口鸡首壶　东晋　高21.2厘米　口径9.0厘米　底径10.1厘米
2002年征集
Celadon pot with dish-shaped mouth chicken-head and two loop handle
rings　Eastern Jin Dynasty
Height21.2cm　Mouth diameter9.0cm　Base diameter10.1cm
Collected in 2002
灰白胎，青釉不及底。浅盘口，束颈，平肩，鼓腹，平底。肩部对称
横置两桥形纽，颈腹部有两道凹弦纹，一端附鸡首，有流，另一端贴
附龙爪鋬手。

青瓷四系盘口壶 东晋 高15.2厘米 口径10.4厘米 底径10.4厘米
2002年4月征集
Celadon pot with dish-shaped mouth and four loop handle rings
Eastern Jin Dynasty
Height15.2cm Mouth diameter10.4cm Base diameter10.4 cm
Collected in April, 2002
灰白胎，青釉不及底。浅盘口，束颈，溜肩，鼓腹，平底。肩部饰三
道凹弦纹和一圈网格纹带，对称置四泥条系，肩腹部饰褐斑点彩。

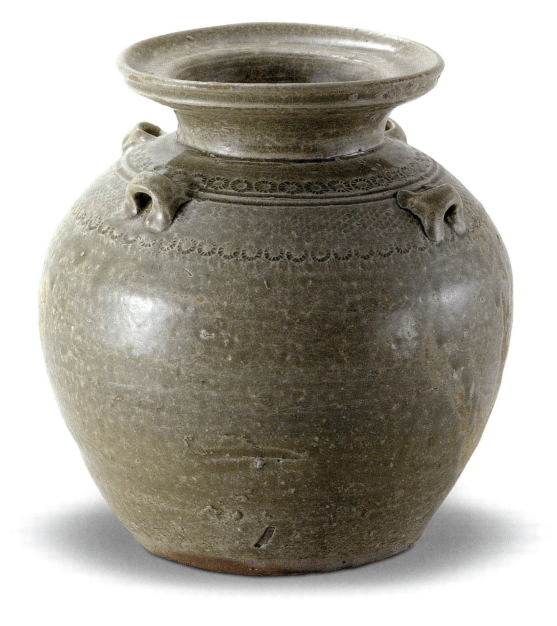

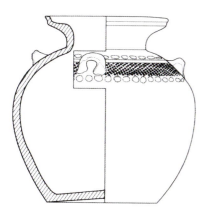

青瓷四系盘口壶　西晋　高16.1厘米　口径10.6厘米　底径10.0厘米
1998年9月马鞍山佳山乡西晋墓出土
Celadon pot with dish-shaped mouth and four loop handle rings
Western Jin Dynasty
Height16.1cm　Mouth diameter10.6cm　Base diameter10.0cm
Unearthed in September, 1998 from a western Jin Dynasty tomb at Jiashan
countryside, Ma'anshan
胎中泛红，青釉不及底。浅盘口，束颈，折肩，弧腹，平底内凹。肩
部饰两圈联珠纹、两道凹弦纹和一圈网格纹组成的纹饰带，对称横置
四泥条系。

青瓷狮形插座 西晋 高9.9厘米 长14.0厘米
1997年4月马鞍山霍里镇西晋墓出土
Celadon lion-shaped holder　Western Jin Dynasty
Height9.9cm　Length14.0cm
Unearthed in April, 1997 from a Western Jin Dynasty tomb at Huoli town,
Ma'anshan

灰白胎，豆青釉。狮呈蹲伏状，昂首，耳呈卷形，双目突出，眉毛弯曲，鼻有两孔，张嘴露齿。面部及颌下贴有胡须，脊中部竖一管状插孔与腹部相通，尾部贴一芭蕉叶尾。腹下部贴有四足，足下刻四爪。通体刻划狮毛，形体瘦长，工艺精湛。

青瓷狮形插座 东晋 高15.0厘米 长15.5厘米 最大腹径12.2厘米
1984年4月马鞍山金家庄区东晋墓出土
Celadon lion-shaped holder   Eastern Jin Dynasty
Height15.0cm   Length15.5cm   Globular belly diameter12.2cm
Unearthed in April, 1984 from an Eastern Jin Dynasty tomb at Jinjiazhuang
district, Ma'anshan
灰白胎，青釉。狮呈蹲伏状，头部捏塑眼、耳、鼻，耳根截有两孔。
张嘴露齿，颌下刻划胡须，脊中部竖一管状插孔与腹部相通，对称处
贴一狮尾，刻划而成。

青瓷唾壶　东晋　高12.0厘米　口径10.6厘米　底径6.2厘米
1986年马鞍山钢铁公司征集
Celadon spittoon　Eastern Jin Dynasty
Height12.0cm　Mouth diameter10.6cm　Base diameter6.2cm
Collected in 1986 at Ma'anshan Iron and Steel Corporation
灰白胎，青黄釉不及底。浅盘口，扁圆腹，平底。

青瓷虎子　东晋　高17.5厘米　口径6.5厘米　底径11.6厘米
1996年1月马鞍山东苑小区东晋墓出土
Celadon Hu-zi vessel　Eastern Jin Dynasty
Height17.5cm　Mouth diameter6.5cm　Base diameter11.6cm
Unearthed in January, 1996 from an Eastern Jin Dynasty tomb
at Dongyuan residential area, Ma'anshan
灰白胎，青釉。仰口，口沿下有两道弦纹。绳状提梁，贴
塑小尾。圆腹，腹上有弦纹两道，底略内凹。

青瓷六系盘口壶 南朝 高31.0厘米 口径15.0厘米 底径11.0厘米
1998年马鞍山当涂县护河镇南朝墓出土
Celadon pot with dish-shaped mouth and six loop handle rings　Southern
Dynasty
Height31.0cm　Mouth diameter15.0cm　Base diameter11.0cm
Unearthed in 1998 from a Southern Dynasty tomb at Huhe town of Dangtu
country, Ma'anshan
灰白胎，青黄釉不及底。深盘口，喇叭颈，圆鼓腹，平底。腹上部对
称横置六桥形系，颈上饰三道凸弦纹。

黄釉条褐彩双系罐　唐　高10.0厘米　口径5.1厘米
底径5.1厘米
1998年10月征集
Yellow-glazed jar with two loop handle rings and brown stripe
design　Tang Dynasty
Height10.0cm　Mouth diameter5.1cm　Base diameter5.1cm
Collected in October, 1998
灰白胎，施黄釉，釉不及底。卷唇，小直颈，椭圆腹，平
底，肩部置对称双系。口及上腹部饰条形褐彩。

黄釉褐彩注子　唐　高9.8厘米　口径4.5厘米　底径4.8厘米
1998年10月征集
Yellow-glazed water dropper with decoration in brown
Tang Dynasty
Height9.8cm　Mouth diameter4.5cm　Base diameter4.8cm
Collected in October, 1998
长沙窑出品，黄釉。喇叭形口，圆腹，平底，腹部有一把
手，对称处有一流，流边点褐彩。

刻花碗 宋 高4.0厘米 口径10.4厘米
底径2.1厘米
1988年9月征集
Porcelain bowl with incised floral design
Song Dynasty
Height4.0cm Mouth diameter10.4cm Base
diameter2.1cm
Collected in September, 1988
灰白胎，影青釉。敞口，尖唇，斜腹，
小圈足，足中有脐。碗内中部有一道凹
弦纹，碗心刻简率的花卉纹。

高足杯 宋 高10.6厘米 口径11.2厘米 底径6.5厘米
2005年12月征集
Porcelain cup with tall stem Song Dynasty
Height10.6cm Mouth diameter11.2cm
Base diameter6.5cm
Collected in December, 2005
胎中泛红，淡青釉，有开片。圆唇，深腹，平底，高
圈足略外撇。

高足杯 宋 高9.6厘米 口径11.0厘米
2005年12月征集
Porcelain cup with tall stem Song Dynasty
Height9.6cm Mouth diameter11.0cm
Collected in December, 2005
灰白胎，淡青釉，有开片。葵口，深腹略外
鼓，底部近平，下承以饼状高足。

托 盏 宋 高8.0厘米 口径10.0厘米
2005年12月征集
Porcelain bowl on a stand Song Dynasty
Height8.0cm Mouth diameter10.0cm
Collected in December, 2005

灰白胎，淡青釉，有开片。葵口，深腹，圈
足。下承以圆形葵口托盘，盘沿上卷，托盘中
部有托圈，底部近平，圈足外撇。

执 壶 宋 高13.4厘米 口径7.6厘米 底径6.6厘米
2005年12月征集
Porcelain Zhihu-pitcher Song Dynasty
Height13.4cm Mouth diameter7.6cm Base diameter6.6 cm
Collected in December, 2005
灰白胎，淡青釉，有开片。圆唇，口呈喇叭状，溜肩，鼓腹，假圈足
略外撇。肩部对称处一端置錾手，另一端有流。

褐彩瓷梅瓶 宋 高16.5厘米 口径3.5厘米 底径5.5厘米
1985年马鞍山霍里镇征集
Porcelain MeiPing-vase with floral design in brown Song Dynasty
Height16.5cm Mouth diameter3.5cm Base diameter5.5cm
Collected in 1985 at Huoli town, Ma'anshan
灰胎，褐彩。圆唇，小口，短直颈，丰肩瘦腹圈足。口、颈、肩部饰
四道褐彩弦纹，腹部饰两个对称的六瓣形开光，内各绘一折枝花，其
外用蕉叶纹填满。

荷叶盖罐 宋 高6.5厘米 口径5.2厘米 底径4.6厘米
1998年10月征集
Porcelain lotus-petal-shaped covered jar　Song Dynasty
Height6.5cm　Mouth diameter5.2cm
Base diameter4.6cm
Collected in October, 1998
灰白胎，影青釉不及底。圆纽，荷叶形盖，圆鼓腹，
平底内凹。

瓷　枕 宋　长25.0厘米 宽17.0厘米 高8.5厘米
1986年征集
Porcelain pillow　Song Dynasty
Length25.0cm　Breadth17.0cm　Height8.5cm
Collected in 1986
灰胎，青绿釉不及底。枕呈长方如意形，面微凹，平
底，长方形后侧面有一个出气孔，整个枕前低后高。
枕面四周刻划波浪纹，中心刻划一朵盛开的牡丹花。

长束腰褐彩瓷枕　宋
高9.6厘米　长22.8厘米　宽12.0厘米
1973年马鞍山当涂县查湾乡宋墓出土
Porcelain contracted waist pillow with brown
decoration　Song Dynasty
Height9.6cm　Length22.8cm　Breadth12.0cm
Unearthed in 1973 from a Song Dynasty tomb
at Zhawan countryside of Dangtu country,
Ma'anshan
吉州窑产品。灰白胎，褐彩。枕呈长束腰
形，一端有气孔，枕内有烧结土。枕部四面
均在褐彩线条框内饰波浪纹，两面对称，两
个端面各饰一朵相同形状的菊花。

水　盂　宋　高11.4厘米　口径16.0厘米
底径6.6厘米
2005年12月征集
Porcelain water container　Song Dynasty
Height11.4cm　Mouth diameter16.0cm
Base diameter6.6 cm
Collected in December, 2005
灰白胎，青黄釉，有开片。圆唇，口微敛，
折肩，弧腹，底内凹。

青花瓷碗　明·天启　高8.8厘米　口径18.0厘米　底径6.4厘米
1995年征集
Blue-and-white porcelain bowl　Tianqi's reign Ming Dynasty
Height8.8cm　Mouth diameter18.0cm　Base diameter6.4 cm
Collected in 1995
敞口，深腹，圈足。内壁上下各施两道弦纹，弦纹间饰葡萄
花纹，内底饰牡丹纹。外部口沿饰两道弦纹，腹部绘满苍松
图。圈足上有四道弦纹，底部书有行楷吉语"长命富贵"。

瓷鼓 明 高38.7厘米 面径22.6厘米 底径23.3厘米
1974年马鞍山当涂县湖阳乡征集
Porcelain drum　Ming Dynasty
Height38.7cm　Top diameter 22.6cm　Base diameter23.3 cm
Collected in 1974 at Huyang countryside of Dangtu country, Ma'anshan
鼓呈腰鼓形。鼓面微凸，饰有双狮盘绣球图案，狮身为黄色，彩球

及四根飞舞的彩带均为孔雀蓝色，绣球中央为一出气孔。鼓身分上、中、下三部分，上下约三分之一处各饰两圈凸出的乳钉纹，乳丁施孔雀蓝釉，中部镂空，主题纹饰为孔雀牡丹，牡丹丛中以太湖石相间。鼓身二分之一处两侧各有一如意形开光图案，内各有一兽头状耳，以连续涡纹表示毛发。整个鼓身中空，底部不施釉。

青花双蝶花卉花浇 清 高13.6厘米 口径26.5厘米 底径17.6厘米
2004年安徽省文物总店征集
Blue-and-white porcelain HuaJiao-ewer with double-butterfly and floral design
Qing Dynasty
Height13.6cm Mouth diameter26.5cm Base diameter17.6 cm
Collected in 2004 from Anhui Province Cultural Relics Head Store
灰白胎，釉色白中泛青。器呈椭圆形，较扁，上部为椭圆形器，长条
形錾手，腹部两厕微向外鼓，平底。盘口内饰对称蝴蝶纹、钱纹，腹
部主题纹为缠枝花卉纹。

后记

　　《马鞍山文物聚珍》在社会各界的支持和本馆同仁的努力下出版发行了。这是我市文博工作的一大幸事。本书浓缩了我市多年来考古发掘、文物征集的重要成果，集中展示了马鞍山地区的悠久历史和璀璨文明。

　　马鞍山是一座传统与现代完美交融的城市。我们骄傲于现代化的钢铁工业，更为那些历史馈赠给我们的文化瑰宝所深深折服。多年来，随着我市社会经济的发展，新的考古发掘成果不断涌现，极大地丰富了馆藏，使得我们的文物种类多、数量丰、等级高，特色鲜明，精品迭出。

　　如何将这些藏于深闺的文物精品更为直观地展现出来，真正做到对文物的"有效保护，合理利用"，一直是我们孜孜追求的目标。本书的编排出版也缘起于此。

　　本书动议早在一九九九年就已提出，却苦于受经费等诸多因素制肘，至今方得实现，其中艰辛不言而喻。尽管困难重重，但全馆同仁从不言弃。没有经费，就凭一股坚毅，倚一份执着，一点一滴积累着；没有经验，就集全馆智慧，参多方资料，一步一步摸索着。

　　通过细致扎实的工作，我们对馆藏文物进行了认真梳理，对蕴藏其间的文化信息进行了深入挖掘，潜心收集、整理了大量的资料。同时，通过积极奔走，取得了社会各方的大力支持。文物出版社不仅在经费上给予我们优惠，还为本书精挑细选了资深摄影师和编辑。在编排中，双方密切配合，反复商讨，几审几校，确保了本书的顺利出版。在定名上，几经斟酌，最终定为《马鞍山文物聚珍》。

　　本书还承蒙安徽省文化厅副厅长李修松、安徽省文物考古研究所研究员张敬国、南京大学教授贺云翱关心指导，担任顾问。李修松和贺云翱先生还分别为本书题了序。在此，谨对关心帮助本书编辑出版的社会各界人士一并致谢！

　　限于文化视野与学术水平，本书在编撰过程中难免挂一漏万。疏漏之处，祈方家指正。

编　者

2006年7月19日

摄　　影：孙之常
　　　　　　赵　勇
英文翻译：江卫艺
英文译审：罗亚琳
装帧设计：李　红
责任印制：王少华
责任编辑：李　红

图书在版编目（CIP）数据

马鞍山文物聚珍/马鞍山市博物馆编，—北京：文物
出版社，2006.9
ISBN 7-5010-1946-0
Ⅰ.马...　Ⅱ.马...　Ⅲ.文物—简介－马鞍山市
Ⅳ.K872.543
中国版本图书馆CIP数据核字（2006）第064554号

马鞍山文物聚珍

马鞍山市文物管理所·马鞍山市博物馆 编
文物出版社出版发行
（北京东直门内北小街2号 邮政编码100007）
http://www.wenwu.com
E-mail:web@wenwu.com
北京图文天地中青彩印制版有限公司制版印刷
新华书店经销
889×1194　1/16　印张：10
2006年9月第一版　第一次印刷
ISBN 7-5010-1946-0/K·1027
定价：180.00元